STUDIO

STUDIO

creative spaces for creative people

SALLY COULTHARD

jacqui
small

This book is dedicated to all the artists, craftspeople and creatives
who bravely let us in to their amazing spaces. You are all wonderful.

First published in 2017 by
Jacqui Small LLP
74–77 White Lion Street
London N1 9PF

Publisher: Jacqui Small
Senior Comissioning Editor: Eszter Karpati
Managing Editor: Emma Heyworth-Dunn
Senior Designer: Rachel Cross
Editor: Sian Parkhouse
Picture Reseach: Sally Coulthard and Caroline Rowland
Production: Maeve Healy

ISBN: 978 1 91025 476 9

A catalogue record for this book is available
from the British Library.

2019 2018 2017
10 9 8 7 6 5 4 3

Printed in China

PAGE 1: In Olaf Hajek's Berlin studio, an
antique plan chest makes a bold statement
and a practical storage solution for finished
illustrations and artwork.

PAGE 2: A converted 1930s shop
on Britain's south coast, Martin O'Neill's
studio is a loosely curated space full of
ephemera and art.

THIS PAGE: For stylist and blogger,
Holly Becker, a vast white cupboard is
the centrepiece of her studio. Like a chef
deciding what to create, Holly can swing
open the doors and look for ingredients,
whether it's a roll of washi tape or a prop
for a photoshoot.

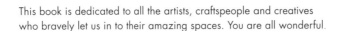
Quarto is the authority on a wide range of topics.
Quarto educates, entertains and enriches the lives of
our readers – enthusiasts and lovers of hands-on living.
www.QuartoKnows.com

CONTENTS

At home, on the farm, there's an old stone barn we rent out to artists. It's a scruffy space, but the people who work there have transformed the building into something truly special.

Not only have the artists organized their studios into useful spaces, they've also created rooms that express who they are and inform the work they produce. Each space reflects the personality of the person who works there – studios are like fingerprints, totally unique. My workspace is the same – it's only an old writing bureau, but it's the place where I sit and write, ponder new ideas and sift through images. It's tiny as workspaces go, but I love it.

The whole process of creating a studio is as important as the work you plan to make in it. A workspace that's well organized and practical is a joy to use. And, it'll make you more productive in the long run. But a studio also has to do something more. Like a virtuous circle, the more of yourself you put into the space, the more your studio will feed your creative drive. Marrying those two elements – the practical and the personal – isn't always easy but, as you'll see in this book, get it right and you'll have a space that not only allows you the freedom to express yourself but also becomes a source of inspiration in its own right.

Creating the perfect studio won't happen overnight. Often you need to work and experiment in a space before you really know what you need. That's how it should be. And, just as your work develops over time, so will your studio. It's a glorious process – one of adding, editing and endless tweaks – but that's half the fun.

FEEL AT HOME A studio should feel like an extension of self. Fill your workspace with decor, colours, books, mementos and personal treasures that act as a source of meaning, inspiration and familiarity.

PEOPLE WHO USE STUDIOS KNOW WHAT SIGNIFICANT SPACES THEY ARE. A studio isn't just a building or a room, it's an acknowledgement that what you are doing is important enough to deserve its own space. If you try and work in a space that isn't fit for purpose or doesn't help your craft, there's a tacit understanding that what you are doing doesn't warrant a proper working environment. It's a kind of self-sabotage.

Poor workspaces make for poor practice, which in turn will thwart any attempts to create something meaningful or high-quality. I learned that early on – my parents, who are both passionate about the arts, had many friends who were artists and craftspeople. As a child, I would accompany them to see their studios and often be allowed to play with the materials and equipment. Even at that age, I could sense how life-affirming these spaces were. These were practical workspaces but they were also a snapshot of a person's personality – some of

FIT FOR PURPOSE If you value your work, value the importance of an effective workspace. Stylist and art director Katrin Bååth's Swedish studio combines elements of creative inspiration with a thoughtful approach to storage, lighting and desk space.

the studios were a riot of colour, eccentric and inviting, others deliciously organized. Some were clearly for heavy, dirty work, full of loud machinery and oily rags; others were gently precise, filled with well-maintained tools and neat storage. What an education for a small child.

GIVE YOURSELF PERMISSION TO HAVE A STUDIO. If you want to write, paint, craft or do anything creative, you need a space that supports your passion. It doesn't have to be grand – a creative spot can be squeezed into almost any room – but it does have to be clearly distinct from all the other spaces you occupy. It also doesn't have to be stuffed to the brim with specialist kit – some of the best studios in this book are those which have been cobbled together from salvaged furniture and household finds. Creative pursuits rarely make millions, so it's always useful to see how other people have found inventive ways to create a workspace on a small budget.

Back home, I've always enjoyed the process of watching new artists settle into the barn and make the space their own. It takes a while for people to get things just right, but when they do, the work flows. I've loved the variety – one artist immediately whitewashed the stone walls and ceiling, and painted the floor a glossy grey, to create a stark backdrop for bright accents and her incredible drawings. Another, a tailor, filled the room with fabric, hung chandeliers and propped vast, boudoir mirrors against the walls to create an intimate sewing den. One space, two totally different approaches.

ELEVATED THINKING It's amazing what you can squeeze into a studio space; in Ariele Alasko's woodworking workshop (left), she has constructed an elevated 'treehouse' office, with plenty of light and simple steps, without compromising any of the workshop's valuable square footage in inner-city New York.

DREAM BIG Experts at manipulating space and props, set designers Amy Lord and Rebekah Whitney turned an unpromising industrial warehouse into a working studio for shoots, meetings and creative consulting (overleaf).

Talking to the artists and craftspeople in this book, many of them said the same thing, that a studio has to be somewhere you actively want to spend time in. It seems an obvious thing to say, but it's actually really profound. Creative people are often deeply affected by their surroundings – any old space simply won't do. The lighting must be right, the colours just so, the furniture and decoration should make you smile. Rarely does an artist have one aesthetic at home and a different one in the studio. There's plenty of crossover, primarily because it's important to feel 'at home' in your favourite workspace.

As you flick through, you'll see that the book is divided into three sections. The first – Studio Inspirations – is designed to give you some ideas for decor so you can create a space that mirrors your personal style. When you make a studio it's important that it not only fits the bill, practically speaking, but that the walls and furniture reflect your aesthetic. There are five distinct looks in this section – it's not the idea that you slavishly copy these studios, but perhaps more that you feel drawn to a particular look and take elements from it that you like. The second section of the book – Studio Work – looks at some of the different ways people are creative and what each activity might require in terms of space and equipment. From draughty lofts to shipping containers, almost any space can be transformed into a studio and I'm envious of the ease with which many artists and craftspeople seem to be able to turn blank spaces into incredible creative hubs. And the third section – Studio Elements – guides you through the practical choices you need to consider to make your space functional and comfortable. There's a lot to think about – from the prerequisites such as power, water and layout, to the fun stuff, such as which style of desk you'd like or how you're going to keep your pencils tidy.

ABSOLUTE BEAUTY Coco Chanel famously said, 'Black has it all. White too. Their beauty is absolute.' Artist and author Lisa Congdon uses an all-white background to do so many things: to keep her studio light, calm and productive, and, above all, to provide a foil for collections of colour.

STUDIOS COME IN ALL SHAPES AND SIZES. From a kitchen table to an industrial unit, an attic room to a garden shed, there's almost no space that can't be used for a creative purpose. If you've got a spare room and you are desperate to get creative, I urge you to go for it. It'll soon become a favourite place. If, like me, you haven't got the space to dedicate an entire room to a studio, take inspiration from all the inventive ways people have carved out a corner for themselves.

Einstein famously said, 'Creativity is contagious. Pass it on.' Being involved in this book has reignited my passion for drawing and painting for pleasure, not just for work projects. If this book inspires you to be creative, and make a space where you can express yourself, then that's the best result I could hope for.

Now, where did I put those pencils ...?

CREATING ILLUSIONS Artists are adept at manipulating their surroundings to create an atmosphere that's conducive to work. Claire Basler's stormy self-painted screen provides decor and drama, and it also achieves the practical purpose of dividing her large studio into cosier sections.

FRONT PORTION
OF BLDG
PRINKLERED

PART ONE
STUDIO INSPIRATIONS

BRIGHT

WHAT COULD BE MORE ENERGIZING THAN BEING SURROUNDED BY VIVID COLOURS? WHETHER IT'S A STUDIO FULL OF CONTRASTING SHADES OR A RIOT OF RAINBOW HUES, IT'S HARD TO BEAT A BRIGHTLY DECORATED WORKSPACE FOR SHEER ENERGY AND CREATIVE EXUBERANCE.

ABOVE LEFT: Few colours are as arresting or brashly optimistic as bright yellow. As with all loud characters, however, they're best in small doses. Here, an egg-yolk yellow chair is nicely balanced with an otherwise simple palette.

ABOVE CENTRE: Colour can be used on every surface – from patterned fabrics to accent walls, painted furniture to self-generated material – creating a patchwork of glorious shades.

ABOVE RIGHT: When it comes to colour, you don't always have to rely on wall paint. Almost every element in your studio can have its own hue, whether it's a bright rug or pot of pencils, a striped flex or a flamboyant filing cabinet.

RETRO PALETTE German
photographer, blogger and stylist
Sylwia Gervais lives and breathes
vivid colours and fifties accents, a
style that's become the signature
for both her work and studio.

WONDERFUL WHITE SPACE Judit
Just's weaving and embroidery
studio (opposite) is a masterclass
in controlled colour. Most of the
colours – hot pinks, reds, oranges,
yellows – sit next to each other on
the colour wheel, creating a vibrant
but harmonious effect. Only the
occasional pop of blue brings the
scheme into contrast.

If you work with colour, you understand its power. You instinctively know that colours create reactions, whether it's unbridled joy or utter gloom. Some combinations of colours stimulate the senses, others make you feel uneasy. And so, if you want a studio that sings with different shades, it's important to handle colour with care. Understanding colour theory, and the way different colours play off each another, allows you to create different effects and moods in your studio.

If you want to use just one strong colour, but in different tints and shades, this is called 'toning'. It's an elegant look but can also be a bit lacklustre if you don't break it up with the odd flash of another colour. If you want a studio that's bursting with energy, use contrasting colours. Contrasting or 'complementary' colours sit directly opposite each other on the colour wheel and putting them together makes for a dramatic and energetic workspace. Go steady though – too many contrasting colours can be overbearing. It's best to pick one dominant colour or use plenty of white space to dilute the effect, a look that lots of the studios in this book have opted for. Alternatively, you can 'harmonize' – this is where you use the colours that sit next to each other on the colour wheel, such as orange, yellow and green. This makes for a visually balanced colour scheme and can work really well if you add in the odd pop of a contrasting colour for lift. Whichever way you choose, don't be afraid to experiment with the amount of colour you use and, if it feels like it's taking over, remember you can always quieten the scheme with a neutral background.

HOME STUDIO

Sarah Campbell, textile designer, UK

For textile designer Sarah Campbell, co-founder of Collier Campbell, and now designing in her own name, the boundary between studio and sitting room has long disappeared. In the living room, fabric samples, fresh paintings and new work create a fluid 'top layer' which ebbs and flows in and out of her apartment.

A few steps away sits Sarah's studio, packed floor to ceiling with storage boxes, paint tubes and works in progress. While both spaces may seem haphazard, Sarah explains, 'on the whole I know what's where – it would be impossible to function otherwise.' There's a practical head on these creative shoulders, a sense that chaos can never be given the upper hand.

A vintage Habitat dining table makes a generous worktable, complete with an old painted chair from Sarah's parents' home. The plan chest and open shelves keep work safely stowed, while a steel trolley holds water jars in case of spillage. 'Everything I need is to hand: it would be hellishly difficult to work if I constantly had to look for the basic tools.'

And Sarah's stroke of genius? Portable inspiration boards. 'I have one wall covered in foamboard which I use for current work, but I also use "travelling" pinboards. I pin references for commissions, new paintings, colour thoughts, to these. I prop them in the studio or in other places to see as I pass – sometimes in my bedroom so I can sleep on the images and look anew when I wake up!'

LIFE'S RICH TAPESTRY It's difficult to know where Sarah Campbell's studio begins and ends. Her workroom might have started life as a separate space at one end of the sitting room, but creativity has a way of creeping out and into every corner. Nowadays, Sarah's glorious fabrics and paintings cover almost every surface – chairs, sofas, floor space and walls.

THE WORKROOM Separated off from the living space by a doorway, Sarah's workroom is filled with storage and the tools of her trade. Most of her design work happens here – painting samples at the large desk – which are then pegged out to dry on a washing line over the plan chest.

LET THERE BE LIGHT When you work with colour, there's no substitute for daylight. Artificial light plays strange tricks, so Sarah makes the most of a bank of large windows that line her London flat (previous pages). There are no curtains, just simple blinds to keep the view clear and the light flooding in. White walls amplify the effect.

SPARE ROOM STUDIO

Paula Mills, illustrator, AUSTRALIA

'My studio looks the way it does because I know no other way of doing it,' explains Paula Mills. It's a simple statement but one that sums up perfectly the relationship between most creatives and their studios; a relationship where a person's artistic vision is so personal and well-defined that there's little difference between their work and their workspace.

If you paint or draw all day, aesthetics matter. But Paula's studio is more than just a colourful workspace, it's the place that bolsters her mood. 'I think it was Alain de Botton who said that aesthetics are fundamental to our well-being.' She continues, 'I feel a whole lot better when I'm surrounded by beautiful, visual stimulation.' There's also a practical side to such an instantly visual space. Working from home, around a busy family, 'I need the stimulation to

HOME COMFORTS People who work from home are adept at juggling. One minute they're in the domestic arena, the next their work zone. For illustrator Paula Mills, having a studio at home, and all its contents laid bare, allows her to grab every spare moment and hit the ground running.

be immediate. If I have a gap in my day and a new range of greeting cards to design, I have to jump right in with ideas for patterns, colours, concepts, etc. I stick things up around me in my studio that I love – be it a colour combination, a piece of hand lettering, an old poster, things which I collect constantly. I also put up work that I am currently busy with – I like to get the work away from my desk and up on a wall to contemplate.'

Colour and pattern reign supreme – pinks, reds and turquoises create a rich patchwork on the walls – but they never overwhelm thanks to Paula's clever use of white, neutrals and clear space. 'In all my travels I have always been struck by how creative us humans can be and how affected we are by beauty,' she muses. 'I suppose my studio space is all about celebrating that.'

MY FAVOURITE THINGS Many creatives like to closely surround themselves with their materials and mementos. For some, it's a function of having a small workspace, but for many, like Paula, it's more than that – it's about creating work surrounded by things of beauty and significance, whether it's your best brushes or a fleamarket treasure.

BASEMENT STUDIO
Judit Just, textile designer, US

There's a theory that repetition is the mother of skill. In other words, keep doing something and eventually you'll grasp it. For textile artist Judit Just, years of learning about colour theory finally seem to have paid off. Through high school, fashion college, sculpture classes and three years studying textiles arts, the repeated emphasis on colour theory honed her visual perception and sensitivity to colour, resulting in an artist who now feels confident enough not just to use colour but to actively play with it.

Originally from Spain, Judit now works from a basement studio in her North Carolina eco home, where she creates her richly coloured wall hangings, tapestries and tactile jewellery. It's not an explosion of colour, but a controlled blast – Judit's expertise with bright colours keep the space, and her work, beautifully balanced. Different kinds of seating and work surfaces come into play depending on the task in hand. From a simple wooden stool to a laid-back mid-century armchair, an old Singer sewing table to a vintage draftsman's desk, Judit can move around the space, weaving one moment, sorting through beads the next. And, when it comes time to sit back and take stock, a vast oxblood Chesterfield provides the perfect resting spot.

FEEL APPEAL For textile artist Judit Just, touch is the most powerful sense. Her colour palette is beautifully bold, but it's the textures of both her work and studio that really sing. From chunky yarns to smooth leather, cold metal to polished floor, her space is almost as layered as her woven wall hangings.

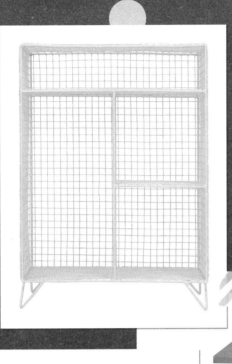

GO BRIGHT

Bright contrasting colours are young, fresh and exuberant, but can leave your studio feeling a bit like a kindergarten. Dull down the effect with dashes of muddied pastels and plenty of white space. Add layers of visual texture with simple graphic patterns – spots, stripes, chevrons – applied in small splashes.

Table legs in primary shades add exclamation marks of strong colour in a white space.

Add strategic bolts of bold colour, such as a bright lampshade or pegboard.

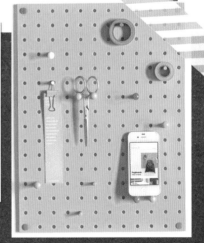

Think about form and colour. Some pieces of furniture and accessories have a strong sculptural quality, adding to the visual rhythm of your studio.

Robust finishes such as enamel, gloss paint or melamine can bring long-lasting shots of bright colour that won't fade over time.

Get down to the details and add tiny dazzling accents, such as stationery or craft materials.

MONO

WHEN YOU STRIP AWAY COLOUR, WHAT'S LEFT? WELL, QUITE A LOT AS IT TURNS OUT. STICKING TO A PARED-DOWN, MONOCHROME PALETTE CAN BE IMMENSELY FREEING, LEAVING YOU TO CONCENTRATE ON OTHER VISUAL ELEMENTS SUCH AS TEXTURE AND DETAIL. FROM INDUSTRIAL GRAPHICS TO RUSTIC PATTERNS, ONE-SHADE SCHEMES CREATE PEACEFUL, ELEGANT SPACES.

ABOVE LEFT: Renoir declared 'the queen of all colours was black'; it's also incredibly powerful, grounding and sophisticated used in a studio space, especially when counterbalanced with crisp white walls and rustic elements.

ABOVE CENTRE: When you erase colour, pattern and detail come to the fore. Here, monochrome newspapers have been layered on the walls to create a visually rich backdrop – the perfect foil for pure-white office furniture.

ABOVE RIGHT: If less-is-more is your natural approach, a black and white studio might just fit the bill. In this Dutch studio, whitewashed walls and stained roof timbers create an impressive statement, without the need for fripperies. Simple furniture and accents complete the look.

Monochrome schemes can have all the elegance of black and white cinematography, so it's perhaps not surprising that so many photographers, film-makers and stylists choose this as their studio decor. When you take away colour, other visual elements come to the fore – such as texture, tone and form – allowing you to view your studio and its contents in a completely different way. If you find colour distracting, monochrome studios can also provide a sense of calm and contemplation, perfect for any creative pursuits that involve writing, thinking or composing.

When you think in monochrome you also have to worry less about the conventions of colour, as long as there's visual balance. Black walls and a white floor? Why not. Black ceiling and a white worktable? Sure. Whatever black takes away, white gives back in terms of light, so gauge how dramatic you want your studio to be and start from that point. If you want a light and bright space, choose white walls and floor, with black accents, every time. Something more intense? Black walls, white accents.

Few studios take the aesthetic in its purest, coldest form – monochrome schemes can be unfriendly spaces so you can soften the edges in a number of ways. Bring in texture, both visual and tactile – everything from a patterned rug to a chunky knit throw will add interest. Add natural notes for warmth – timber work surfaces, stone floors, linens and wool. Try breaking the monotony with just the tiniest splash of one colour – perhaps a favourite work chair or pinboard. Or bling it back to life with shiny surfaces, chandeliers and other sparkly accents.

SITTING ROOM SPACE
Tenka Gammelgaard, painter, DENMARK

What separates true artists from people who are just playing at it? One word: commitment. Being totally and utterly driven, focused and relentless when it comes to their work. For some, it involves exploring the same images, concepts or motifs again and again. For others, it's all about the process – gathering, sorting, collating material, repeating the same creative actions. For Danish artist Tenka Gammelgaard, all these apply. This is an artist who has taken a commitment to working only in monochrome to a gloriously extreme level. The studio she works in, the art she forges, the clothes she wears (she only wears white during the summer and black in the winter), the materials she uses, the tools, the house she inhabits – absolutely everything is black and white. Even her paintbrushes have been carefully painted with black and white stripes.

With a background in theatre scenery, it's clear Tenka thinks about the backdrop to her work as much as her art. In fact, the backdrop is part of her art. It's difficult to unpick where the studio ends and her art begins – black splashes on the white floor, black paintbrushes stuffed in tin cans like rows of flowers, black paint in tiny white bowls – all these elements create a stage, a chic interior and a buzzing workspace all in one.

GREY AREAS Occupying the space that would otherwise be the living room, Tenka Gammelgaard's Copenhagen home studio is an art installation in itself. Her commitment to black and white extends everywhere – black storage boxes, white desk, black lighting, white flooring and walls. The only other 'colour' – metallic grey silver – acts as a mirror, reflecting and multiplying the monochrome effect. Even the paint splatters, used brushes and stacked pots become part of the monochrome scheme.

STYLIST'S WORKSPACE
Katrin Bååth, stylist, SWEDEN

Stylists are alchemists. They take everyday objects and transform them into something extraordinary. They understand balance and composition as well as any artist. They appreciate the importance of visual rhythm as much as any architect. And they have a photographer's understanding of form and pattern. Bring these three disciplines together, combine them with an interior designer's flair for space and colour, and you've got the recipe for a visually stunning studio.

Art director and stylist Katrin Bååth's workspace is a masterclass in careful editing. With a clean, white background and just a few, well-chosen pieces, she's created a studio that's crisp, sleek and just ever-so-edgy. It's the simple things that matter here the most.

'The windows, the view and the amazing light are the best parts of my studio,' explains Katrin. 'I decided to keep it monochrome and made a promise to myself to only buy furniture that I really loved.' The centrepiece, a black cabinet from Lindebjerg Design, is a practical storage space for props, but also a beautiful display in its own right and Katrin's favourite piece in the studio.

In a stylist's world, everything can be adapted or altered to create something new and exciting. A plain IKEA sideboard is transformed with a bespoke marble top, a clothes hanger is made from leather belts and a simple rod, and a mirrored hostess trolley becomes stylish storage. Vintage pieces rub shoulders with cutting-edge Swedish design to create a studio that's relaxed, chic and couldn't be anyone else's but Katrin's.

WELL-ORDERED SERENITY Near the station in Jönköping, Sweden, sits an old restored matchstick factory. With its vast windows, high ceilings and views of Lake Vatten, it's Katrin Bååth's treasured studio and the space she feels at her most creative (opposite and overleaf). Clean lines, a limited palette and well-chosen pieces make a sleek, sophisticated statement without scrimping on the studio essentials, such as a generous work desk, ample lighting and good seating.

PERSONAL STYLING Katrin's props become studio decor and vice versa (this page). Monochrome paintings and photographs, vintage props and an old drinks trolley laden with favourite finds provide visual texture and bring in a sense of 'home'.

GO MONO

Without the distraction of colour, texture and pattern have a chance to shine. Get the most from a monochrome studio by adding bags of different visual and physical texture – coarse surfaces, touchy-feely fabrics, shiny or reflective accents. Create interest with pattern – bold graphic statements or smaller, more intricate designs work equally well. Add the odd natural element to soften the look.

Patterns add visual texture so don't be afraid to mix chevrons, stripes, spots, ikat and checks.

A little black goes a long way. For a light, bright workspace, keep the walls and floors white and add drama with dark statement pieces.

Metallic accents, such
as mesh or galvanized
steel, add tonal variety
to the scheme

Lighting brings the monochrome
look to life. Choose shades and
lamps with an inherent sculptural
quality - ones that look as good
switched off as on.

NATURAL

FEW THINGS ARE AS INSPIRING AS MOTHER NATURE. FOR SOME ARTISTS, IT'S HER GEOMETRY AND NATURAL PATTERN MAKING. FOR OTHERS, IT'S NATURE'S RANDOM CHAOS, RAW POWER OR INHERENT FRAGILITY THAT MOVE PEOPLE TO CREATE IN HER HONOUR. WHATEVER YOUR MOTIVE, SURROUNDING YOURSELF WITH PLANTS, ANIMALS AND NATURAL INSPIRATION CAN HELP YOUR WORK GROW.

ABOVE LEFT: Linda Felcey works from a shepherd's hut in an old orchard, surrounded with willow and poplar trees. Being immersed in the landscape inspires and informs her paintings and provides a peaceful spot to work uninterrupted.

ABOVE CENTRE: French artist Claire Basler lives and works in a chateau, where the vast room proportions can accommodate not only her paintings and murals but also the plants that inspire her work.

ABOVE RIGHT: The warehouse studio of mid-century furniture restorer Cadence Hays is light, bright and full of houseplants and cut foliage.

Artists have long been fascinated with the natural world. From the earliest cave paintings, humans have always wanted to create art that says something profound about our relationship with the environment. For some artists and craftspeople, it's important to get out into the outdoors, but for others it's equally significant to bring nature back to the studio. And whether it's found objects from a beach stroll or huge swathes of living branches, there are plenty of ways you can create a studio inspired by nature.

Natural materials are key when it comes to walls, floors and furniture – gently worn woods, linens, stone and glass are all part of this aesthetic. Colours are often muted – not that nature can't be garish, but greens, off-whites, greys and soft blues provide a more sympathetic backdrop to any nature-inspired work. Nature is also a great provider of free decor, so make the most of any found materials – flowers, twigs, cones, seeds, pebbles, driftwood, grasses, shells, feathers, bones and so on. How glorious that these raw materials just so happen to make beautiful interior accents. You can deal with all this variety in whatever way you choose – some studio owners neatly categorize their natural finds like a Victorian specimen collector, others allow nature to grow and colonize the space.

And don't be afraid to change your studio with the seasons – part of being inspired by nature is that you enjoy and appreciate its transitions. How different a studio might be in the mid-flurry of spring from the sleepy decline of autumn.

ELEMENTS OF NATURE Organic inspiration can come in many forms. From choosing a natural palette of paint colours – sky blues, earth tones and gentle greens – to filling a moodboard with organic materials and shades as Heather Ross has done (opposite above). Some artists take it one step further and literally bring the outdoors in; here, cut flowers and coppiced branches bring life and visual movement to workspaces (this page).

CHATEAU STUDIO
Claire Basler, painter, FRANCE

If you want to paint nature you have two choices: take your easel outdoors or, as Claire Basler often does, bring the outdoors to you. In her extraordinary studio, in a 13th-century castle in central France, Château de Beauvoir, the line between inside and out has been blurred. Huge branches and bucketfuls of flowers transform the studio into a 'living space', a forest of inspiration for Claire to translate onto canvas.

But these aren't sweet little still-lifes. Claire's cathedral-like canvases explore ideas of strength and fragility, how nature can both be all powerful and paper delicate. To capture these ideas in paint, Claire surrounds herself with plants on a vast scale, allowing them to 'grow' and creep beyond the studio and into the home, taking over walls, ceilings and floor spaces along the way.

With its high ceilings and huge glazed arched windows, the studio has the feel of a glasshouse, filled with plants and flooded with sunshine. For some painters, such direct light would provide a challenge but not Claire: 'The light and shadows change from day to evening, and through the seasons. The studio is never the same two days in a row.'

NATURE'S GRAND SCALE One thing artist Claire Basler is not short of is space. In the grounds of her medieval chateau, you'll find her working away in the empty outbuildings that once housed the orangerie and stables.

The light is also muted by Claire's clever use of greys. From pale walls to the charcoal furniture, her palette of grey not only calms but also helps her focus. 'I never keep furniture or floors wood colour, unless they're really dark,' Claire explains. 'If wood is too yellow or too red, it catches my eye and often disrupts how I "read" my paintings. I love the colours of iron and cement – they seem to vibrate with the light – and provide a contrast to the delicacy of the flowers.'

THE VIEW BEYOND Their grand proportions and vast arched windows of the studio are perfect for Claire's huge canvases and tall cuttings of foliage and, better still, allow her unparalleled views of the garden and landscape beyond.

SHEPHERD'S HUT STUDIO

Linda Felcey, painter, UK

Linda Felcey experiences the world through its seasons. A painter inspired by wild, uncultivated gardens, native English woodland and ancient hedgerows, she works immersed in a sense of place and environment. When the weather's clement, she might venture out to work *en plein air,* but more often than not you can find her in the orchard, tucked away in a beautifully crafted shepherd's hut.

'I've always worked directly in the landscape. When my children were born I made the decision to focus all my energies on the family and my personal creative output slowed to a minimum. As they grew up and became more independent, my husband designed and built me this studio as a thank-you and to encourage me back out into the landscape so I could re-engage with myself as an artist.'

Everything about the studio is designed to allow Linda to re-connect with her natural surroundings: 'Built from English oak, insulated with lambs' wool and warmed by a small wood-burning stove,' Linda explains, 'it provides the warmest and safest of retreats. The windows slide back into a cavity within the studio walls allowing the smells and sounds of nature to permeate the space. The studio shares a unique and intimate relationship with the landscape, which is truly conducive to the creative spirit.'

And best of all? It's a studio that can move with the seasons. When a copse of crack willow bursts into life or the reed beds begin to stir, Linda can simply pull up the steps to her shepherd's hut and roll on to enjoy new and ever-changing views and vistas.

WORKSPACE ON WHEELS If, like Linda Felcey, your work is all about being immersed in the landscape, there can be no better choice of studio than a shepherd's hut. Linda's wheeled workspace nestles quietly outside, among the subject-matter that inspires her work. The hut's Quaker-like simplicity is a huge part of its charm and effectiveness as a workspace; a pared-back interior of oak, wainscoting and honest furniture keeps the focus outward and beyond, into the orchard.

SUBJECT TO NATURE Linda often brings natural elements into her space – lichen-covered branches, buds and blossom, which she paints against the old pottery that she's collected. Simple pegs and a line allow her to hang sketches around the space.

A COSY RETREAT Regardless of the season, Linda lights a fire in the wood burner as her first ritual of the working day. On the stove sits a Japanese cast-iron kettle ready to make tea, which will vary from nettle to lime flower depending on what Linda gathers en route.

GO NATURAL

Nature is the greatest designer. Find inspiration in the patterns and textures of organic forms – from huge floral prints to rustic antlers, botanical fabrics to living greenery. Steer clear of synthetics such as neons and shocking brights – they can jar against nature's muted, earthy palette. Off-whites, greens, blue greys and earthy darks all work well alongside sun-bleached woods, rustic fabrics and natural-fibre rugs.

Focus on elements that echo the natural aesthetic: wood, cane, bamboo and other naturally sourced materials.

NOTES

Botanical prints add a curated feel
to your studio - display in ordered
groups for maximum impact.

Pull together mismatched
floral stationery for a
blousy, vintage vibe.

Look for furniture constructed
of salvaged wood to add a
rustic, well-worn note.

Bring in houseplants, botanical
accents and statement pieces
inspired by organic forms.

INDUSTRIAL

CREATIVE PEOPLE ARE OFTEN DRAWN TO INDUSTRIAL SPACES; IT'S
A DEMOCRATIC, UNSHOWY AESTHETIC, ONE THAT CHIMES WITH
PEOPLE WHO PREFER PURPOSE TO PRETTINESS. BUT THAT DOESN'T
MEAN INDUSTRIAL STUDIOS CAN'T BE BEAUTIFUL, ESPECIALLY WHEN
YOU EMPLOY HONEST MATERIALS AND PRACTICAL DESIGN ON
A GRAND SCALE.

ABOVE LEFT: The industrial look can be a serious, no-nonsense affair, but if your heart aches for a bit of colour it's an aesthetic that's easily lightened with bright and bold strokes of different hues.

ABOVE CENTRE: A few carefully edited industrial accents – a factory chair or metal filing cabinet – can instantly inject a sense of stylish utility.

ABOVE RIGHT: A sturdy bench, the absolute lynchpin of an industrial studio, takes centre place in a knife-making workshop.

It's a design cliché, the struggling artist living and working in a disused factory, but there's plenty to praise about studios that embrace an industrial vibe. It's a masculine aesthetic – filled with hardworking materials and clean edges – but the most successful spaces combine tough utility and softer, organic notes. At the heart of the look is an appreciation of honest materials and things built for purpose. Bare bricks, concrete, exposed metalwork – there's beauty in these plain-speaking elements. Factory furniture – which is often functional and pleasingly simple – adds to the look; scout around for studio elements such as canteen tables, trestles, lockers, steel chairs, wire storage racks – you know the drill. Industrial studio spaces are often large scale, so enjoy the freedom of choosing over-sized worktables, storage cupboards and salvaged decor. Lighting will also need to be bold, but don't opt for strip fluorescents – they're too harsh to work under. Runs of lights look effective – multiple factory pendants, barn lights, caged light bulbs, bulkheads and enamel shades all hit the spot.

And don't just go for vintage. The concept of utility furniture was originally about creating tough, well-designed pieces that made efficient use of scarce resources. Lack of fussiness, good-quality materials and basic but elegant construction are still principles that work if you're choosing furniture for an industrially inspired studio. Exposed copper water pipes, brass bib taps, stone or Belfast (butler) sinks, metal surface-mounted switches and sockets (outlets) – even your utilities can add to this uncomplicated, no-frills look.

FACTORY FUNDAMENTALS

There are some absolute must-haves if you want to embrace the industrial look in your studio. Caged lights or enamel pendants, exposed brickwork, robust cermic sinks and brass bib taps and (opposite) metal staff lockers are all key elements for the look. The more battered and lived-in the better.

ARTS CENTRE STUDIO
Aaron Ruff, jewellery designer, US

Don't be fooled by the sparkles and shine. At its heart, jewellery-making is a rugged, hand-beaten craft, hammering and persuading metals to bend at your will. So it's fitting, perhaps, that the Brooklyn studio of Digby & Iona's Aaron Ruff is about as masculine and industrial as you can get, filled not only with the tools of his trade, but also nautical, military and mechanical finds.

Exposed brick walls and dark woods provide the perfect backdrop for Aaron's ever-evolving collection of heirloom finds. Everything from vintage industrial lamps and classic motorcycles to flags and folk art fill the space, providing inspiration for his latest creations. Shelves, reclaimed filing cabinets and utility drawers offer much-needed storage for Aaron's treasures, while chunky timber benches, worklamps and simple stools create a practical workspace.

With a background in carpentry and furniture design, Aaron is clearly fascinated by raw materials and construction, a passion that plays out in his studio and his work. But there's also a strong sense of nostalgia, an affinity with objects that have had a past life or beg to be collected. It's an aesthetic that suits the industrial look – objects with a history always sit well in a space that's got its own story to tell. And what a story the building has – a 19th-century factory that, in its heyday, manufactured novelty 'invisible dog leads' in their thousands and now, in its second incarnation, houses some of New York's finest artists and craftspeople.

WORKSHOP WITH A STORY What is it about old manufacturing spaces that make such good studios? For jewellery designer and maker Aaron Ruff, it must be that potent mix of practical, functional surroundings and the hit of history that comes when you occupy a space in former toy factory that's been transformed into a vibrant arts centre. The walls, floors and contents resonate with past industry, which in turn, feeds into Aaron's designs. Rather than fight the industrial aesthetic, Aaron has added to it and made it his own with his ever-evolving collection of salvaged furniture, factory lighting and battered memorabilia.

WAREHOUSE WORKSPACE
Catherine Derksema, textile designer, AUSTRALIA

For Cath Derksema, her studio is a love affair. 'My workspace is my world away from my world,' she explains. 'It's a pure response to my emotional and spiritual needs – a place where I feel completely safe, a place that is continually evolving, changing and inspiring me every day.'

When you work in an environment to which you feel so connected, every element – even tools – becomes significant. 'My paintbrushes are like old friends who have been with me through thick and thin,' she smiles. 'They definitely have personalities and I love giving them a voice. I also surround myself with plants, shells, collected artefacts from travels, yarn, twine, threads and anything that evokes a rich, playful memory.'

In fact, almost everything is on display, feeding the creative process and inspiring new ideas. Books, magazines and other reference materials teeter in stacks around the studio, wire baskets overflow with colourful yarns and fabrics, and rescued pieces of furniture find sanctuary in Cath's industrial space. Two old worktables are particular favourites; 'They were rescued when the local school closed its art room and have wonderful childlike markings and graffiti on them.'

'When I first moved into the studio it was a very raw, semi-industrial warehouse space. I didn't want to change its history as I loved the light, the floorboards, the old windows, its essence. From the ground up, I knew it was the space for me.' Sounds like a match made in heaven.

BIG, BOLD & BEAUTIFUL It can be difficult to make a large studio feel cosy, especially an old warehouse, but for textile designer and artist Cath Derksema, her workspace is nothing short of perfect. Huge windows and double-height open ceilings give the studio a cathedral-like sense of peace and plenty of room to manoeuvre large rolls of fabric. Work surfaces are key in Cath's studio – not just for designing and printing her bespoke fabrics, but also for demonstrating techniques at workshops. From pallet wall storage and old clothes racks to a dye-splattered cast-iron bath for rinsing fabrics, there's a real sense that this is a pretty but ultimately productive space.

MILL WORKSHOP
Benjamin Edmonds, knife maker, UK

With a skill as raw and hazardous as knife-making you'd imagine creating a good-looking workspace would be low on the list of priorities. Benjamin Edmonds' Blok Knives workshop, however, demonstrates that even in the most functional building you can forge a space that's both practical and personal.

The space started life as an outbuilding for the historic cotton mill next door. Keen to strip it back to its bare shell, Ben exposed the brickwork and roof void, showcasing the original beams and tiles. 'We've tried to keep a very industrial feel to the space,' explains Ben. 'After all, we are knife makers. But I also wanted to be sympathetic to the building, so we had electrics installed in metal conduit, and hung lights from beams. The floor is simply painted to show all the lumps and bumps of previous use.'

Form follows function, so Ben had to be practical about layout. 'We use lots of machines so making them accessible and safe to use was paramount.' Deciding on a linear set-up, Ben placed workbenches around the outside with a large table in the middle. 'We have a process that flows around the workshop so we all know at which stage a knife is at.' But it's not all about pure utility: 'I installed a log burner, as there's nothing like that smell and sound. I'm a big believer in having a space to relax, somewhere to take yourself away to when you're not working.'

INDUSTRIOUS SPACE At no point in its long life was this brick building designed for anything but graft and industry. Functional to its core, but also beautiful, the space is ideal for a craft that involves both intricacy and heavy machinery. Ben's kept true to its honest, unfussy architecture, but also personalized the space with branded lighting, battered furniture and a wood-burning stove. Industrial lighting – enamel pendants and caged light bulbs – supplement the natural light that streams in through the ground-floor windows.

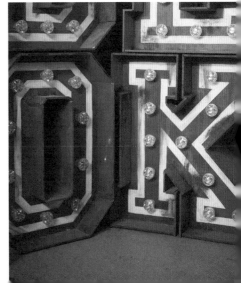

GO INDUSTRIAL

Exposed brickwork, planked floors, bare concrete and galvanized metals – the fundamentals of the industrial look. Furniture needs to be solid, unfussy and utilitarian. Colour comes from your raw materials – steel greys, worn wood and aged bricks – but if it's all getting too factory floor, inject a bit of creativity in the form of large-scale artworks and bright accents.

Add character and an irreverent twist with oversized fonts and commercial artwork.

Trolleys, lockers and other factory finds double up nicely as studio essentials.

Industrial swivel stools are perfect for working on surfaces at variable heights.

Both practical and sculptural, caged lights have become the byword for industrial chic.

Look out for vintage pieces with shelves, racks and castors - fantastically practical for the modern studio.

Choose a workbench or trestle table that's sturdy and unfussy, with a surface that can withstand a beating.

Table lamps from repurposed industrial components can add a quirky edge.

COLLECTED

IF YOUR ART OR CRAFT INVOLVES SIFTING THROUGH COUNTLESS OBJECTS AND IMAGES, IT'S IMPOSSIBLE TO WORK IN A STERILE STUDIO – YOU NEED TO SURROUND YOURSELF WITH THE THOUSANDS OF THINGS THAT INSPIRE AND INFORM YOUR WORK. CREATIVE CLUTTER IS PRICELESS – IT'S THE FUEL THAT FEEDS YOU – BUT THE TRICK IS TO STOP IT SPILLING OVER AND SPOILING YOUR FUN.

ABOVE LEFT: Designer Nathalie Lété finds inspiration by gathering and displaying souvenirs from her childhood, fairytale imagery and child-sized furniture.

ABOVE CENTRE: The large red cabinet in Emily Sutton's studio was the first piece of furniture she bought for it. Over the following five years she's stuffed it with treasures from far and wide, and its contents are ever present in her still-life paintings and illustration work.

ABOVE RIGHT: Collage artist Martin O'Neill takes a traditional approach to his work, keeping digital involvement to a minimum. The result is a studio filled with vintage papers, postcards and found objects, all waiting patiently to be cut out, glued and given a new context.

People who enjoy the process of gathering, collating and displaying things also need to be good curators. Clutter can be glorious, but only if you feel that you have some semblance of control. For some, the act of collecting and organizing is part of their art practice, for others it's a rich source of visual inspiration and ideas. Whatever the motive, spaces filled with curios are dazzling and just a little bit dangerous. You're never far from the sense that collecting will spill over into hoarding – there are often so many objects, you can't quite take it all in. And that's why they're such exciting spaces.

But studios also have to function. Take inspiration from other professions that display and work with large numbers of small objects, such as specimen collectors, printers, haberdashers, stationers, natural history curators and ephemera buffs. Curiosity cabinets, plan chests, printers' trays, glass-fronted display cases, collectors' cupboards, miniature drawers and architects' filing systems are all handsome storage options. Don't be afraid to layer the storage – stack cupboard upon cupboard, drawers upon drawers. Other flat surfaces can be brought into use as display areas – shelves, mantelpieces and bookcases.

Part of the logic of this look is that your visual inspiration is so immediate and varied. Don't hide things away – cover your walls and doors with images, display your tools and materials, and surround yourself with work past and present. It's hard not to feel motivated when you step into your studio and are hit with such a visual blast.

WALL-TO-WALL INSPIRATION
Many well-known artists are or were collectors. Andy Warhol famously kept box upon box of kitsch consumer culture and personal effects, while Joseph Cornell turned assemblage into an art form. Graphic artist Martin O'Neill (above), illustrator Emily Sutton (right) and designer Nathalie Lété (far right), all collect and display archives of found objects, essential to the making of their own work.

SPLIT-LEVEL STUDIO
Nathalie Lété, designer, FRANCE

In a studio on the ground floor of a suburban Parisian block, Nathalie Lété's creative spirit flows with gleeful abandon. It's a space that's ever evolving – one year painted green, the next year pink – but one thing remains the same: it's a space that's colourful, curated and completely idiosyncratic.

'I bought this studio 15 years ago,' explains Nathalie. 'I haven't done much, just insulated the walls and put down a layer of concrete on the ground. I have a mezzanine floor with a bedroom and bathroom as well as my office . . . it's more cosy and homely upstairs.'

It's the perfect split-level space for Nathalie to create her work. Large windows along one wall flood the studio with light. 'I'm lucky to have plenty of space; it means I can leave my work stations as they are, without having to tidy them away each time. I can also flit from one technique to another.'

Like a magpie collecting for her nest, she pulls elements from far and wide – folk imagery, outsider art, children's fairytales – and weaves them into her own unique designs.

For some people, their studio is more than just a workspace. It's an escape. It's the space where you don't have to compromise. For Nathalie Lété, like a child creating her own fairytale world, it's the place she's 'totally free'.

TREASURE TROVE With so many trinkets, Nathalie has to be curator-like about her storage and work surfaces. Everything from industrial drawers to bespoke cube-cupboards, fleamarket shelves to a heavy carpenter's table, keep clutter contained but always visually accessible.

UPSTAIRS DOWNSTAIRS Having a mezzanine floor allows Nathalie some respite from the studio floor, but also gives her a unique view of her work (overleaf). In a smaller studio, she wouldn't have this bird's-eye view of her work – changing perspective can reveal new ideas as well as dig up challenges.

ONE HOUSE TWO STUDIOS
Mark Hearld & Emily Sutton, artist & illustrator, UK

In a tall, thin Georgian townhouse in the centre of York, one of the UK's most talented creative couples jostle for studio space. While Mark Hearld, artist and printmaker, busily squirrels away in the attic, on the next floor down, illustrator Emily Sutton is concentrating on her latest commission.

'In terms of our working styles,' explains Emily, 'I am much more of a planner, and work in a methodical and meticulous way. Mark is an improviser; expressive and spontaneous and enjoys creating on the spot from the materials around him. These differences are reflected in the look of our studios – mine being fairly neat and tidy and Mark's is perpetually in creative chaos!'

But for all the superficial differences, both Mark and Emily's work is shaped by their incredible archive of curios. 'Mark has always been the prime collector and, as he had already had a flat before we moved in together, the majority of objects were from his own collection. My interest in objects is based on things that I like to include in my drawings and paintings, so my studio is filled with a random mixture of inspiring postcards and bits of ephemera, old toys, transfer ware plates and Victorian tins. I have a large red cabinet in my studio that was the first piece of furniture I bought for it.'

THE IMPROVISER AND THE ORGANIZER
While artist Mark Hearld's attic studio is a non-stop creative whirlwind (below), his partner Emily Sutton takes a more methodical approach to her workspace (right). Over the past five years, Emily has filled her studio with treasures collected from places as far afield as Paris, Tuscany and America, along with more local finds.

COLLECTORS' CABINET Emily's antique lacquer-red cupboard provides valuable storage space for her favourite still-life subjects but it's also been the subject of a watercolour painting itself. The contents are constantly being used in her still-lifes and as inspiration for her illustrations.

OLD SHOP STUDIO
Martin O'Neill, collage artist, UK

There's often a fine line between collecting and hoarding. Martin O'Neill even describes the studio he shares with his wife Jackie Parsons as 'part workshop, part landfill' and yet it wouldn't be fair to describe the contents of his space as anything less than a glorious, working archive.

Martin is a collage artist. In a converted 1930s seafront shop, he surrounds himself with a vast collection of objects, ephemera and collage material. They're the raw ingredients of his work, the parts that make up the whole, but they're also a meta-collage of their own.

'We don't have pinboards,' Martin explains, 'but an ever-changing range of artefacts and accoutrements that adorn the walls, shelves and desk spaces; these could be artworks in progress, clear bags of collected collage material stuck up with bulldog clips, or small individual cut-outs, stuck onto a wall. These objects, bags and bits migrate around the space depending on what projects are being worked on – a cross-pollination starts to occur when you work on various things at once.'

Everything is an assemblage. Desktops heave with found and self-generated collage material. Shelves sag with mementos and curios. Martin's storage is an artwork in itself and keeps the clutter tightly controlled; from vintage margarine boxes and letterpress trays to plan chests and shoe boxes. Hand-scribbled labels show a Victorian collector's sense of order cut with a graffiti artist's wit and edge. How apposite, then, that even the building itself has a collaged history, with past lives as diverse as a junk shop, travel agent, art gallery and furriers.

THE ARTIST AS COLLECTOR The raw material of any collage is an archive of fragments. Creating a system that's both logical and inspiring is no mean feat but Martin O'Neill's studio is testament to his ability to keep order when chaos is so near at hand. The walls, shelves and desks are covered with artworks in progress, bags of collage material and small individual cut outs.

STACKS OF STORAGE Martin's vast archive of collage material is kept in everything from old plan chests to shoe boxes. Open bookshelves, desktop files, metal filing cabinets, commercial packaging and index files are also full to the brim (overleaf).

Martin O'Neill

Series title / Die Zusammensetzung

Works / 1 - 20

IT ALL
MAKES
SENSE

GENERAL

GO COLLECTED

Patterned papers, bright wall colours or plastering your studio with images will create the busy background you need. Mix open storage and shelves with glass-fronted cupboards, plan chests and printers' trays. Have a theme or organizing principle behind your displays to stop the studio looking like landfill. Grouping things by colour, type, age, purpose or material can unite a disparate crowd of objects.

Glass-fronted cabinets are a neat storage solution and add a hint of the specimen-hunter.

Fleamarket furniture, old ephemera and themed finds pull together to create the collector's look.

Collaged pattern
gives depth and
visual texture –
even your choice of
lighting can add
another layer.

PERIODENSYSTEM DER ELEMENTE
KURZPERIODENSYSTEM

Curiosities and statement
pieces that are either
rare or unusual, add a
deliciously eccentric
undertone.

PART TWO
STUDIO WORK

CRAFTS

WHEN WE THINK OF 'CRAFTS' WE OFTEN CONJURE UP IMAGES OF CROCHETED TEA CADDIES AND WOBBLY POTTERY, BUT THE REALITY IS THAT THE CRAFT WORLD IS FULL OF HIGHLY SKILLED MAKERS, CREATING EVERYTHING FROM EXQUISITE JEWELLERY TO BESPOKE CABINETRY. IT JUST SO HAPPENS THEIR STUDIOS ARE PRETTY FANTASTIC TOO.

ABOVE LEFT: A corner of Cadence Hays' light and airy furniture studio, which she's filled with stacks of collected pottery and living plants, and shares with other artists, painters and potters.

ABOVE CENTRE: Gavin Rookledge creates exquisite hand-made books and artefacts bound in leather, vellum and suede in his workshop Rook's Books. Everything that's made in his London studio is handcrafted the traditional way, using antique tools and techniques.

ABOVE RIGHT: French ceramic artist Lise Meuiner uses timelessly simple tools and a gentle palette of glazes to create her beautiful decorative pieces from her Paris live/work studio.

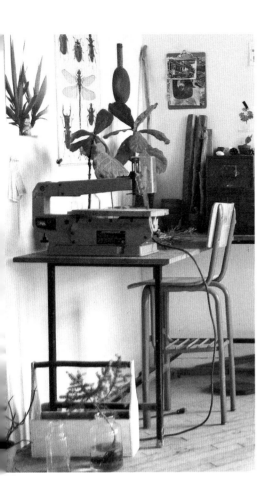

An increasing number of people make a living from craft; there's been a real resurgence of interest for handmade, handcrafted objects. Mass-produced products often lack soul, while crafted items are full of character and human personality. There's also a thrill to be had from owning an object you know to be the only one of its kind.

'Craft' as a term covers so many different disciplines, many of which need specific working environments. Ceramics and glass work, for example, can demand large workspaces, ready to cope with heat, water and industrial equipment. Leatherwork, stone masonry, wood carving are all crafts that need dry, simple spaces with plenty of hand-tool storage and sturdy benches. Decoupage, book binding, paper cutting – delicate, intricate work that thrives in a neat environment with immaculate work surfaces and a rigorous system for filing paper and off-cuts.

With such a vast range of activities coming under one umbrella term it can be tricky to say anything meaningful about how to make the ideal craft studio. However, with most crafts one of the biggest problems is imposing some kind of organization onto a wide range of materials. Unlike fine art, which tends to involve (although by no means exclusively) one type of material, crafting often involves different stages and a multitude of materials and tools. Whether it's piles of coloured paper, buckets of beads, pottery glazes or rows of inks, nothing spoils a crafting studio more than chaos.

With that in mind, whatever craft you choose, the first consideration has to be finding a dedicated space that can be permanently occupied. You can't do craft professionally if you have to keep packing up and moving spaces. If you make things from home, crafts also have a way of spreading into other living areas, so it's important to be ruthless about choosing a spot and sticking to it. That doesn't mean you can't craft in a room designed for another purpose – kitchen tables are a favourite spot for many crafters in the early stages of a business – but at the very least it's important to have dedicated storage for all your kit.

If you opt for the corner of a room, consider some method of screening – not only does this mean you don't have to clear away at the end of every craft session but, more importantly, you can also work undistracted by your domestic surroundings. Lots of things can act as a screen: a double-sided bookcase, a folding room divider, curtains, vertical blinds, even a large framed canvas. Crafting cupboards are also an option and have the added advantage of closable doors to hide all your supplies when not in use. The key element when choosing a crafting cupboard (or converting a wardrobe) is to have some kind of pull-out or drop down desk, otherwise your working space is too limited, but the potential for adding shelving, boxes, pinboards, hanging hooks and tool storage is endless.

As a general rule, craft spaces work best when you keep floor spaces as clear as possible (so you can work safely), have generous work surfaces, and keep materials and tools stored where they can be quickly accessed. Wall-mounted storage is particularly useful – not only does it keep the floor space uncluttered but it also makes browsing for materials easier. Few things are more frustrating than opening and closing endless boxes stacked on top of each other, so think about combining open storage, such as shelves and cubby holes, with hanging storage and pegboards, and sets of drawers.

Desk spaces and work surfaces should be as generous as possible – long runs of trestle tables or multiple smaller desks can help you zone different activities without having to constantly pack away mid-make. In terms of floor surfaces, keep them smooth. You'll be constantly sweeping or vacuuming, so small lightweight rugs will soon start to get annoying and thick carpets unmanageable. If you want to soften a hard floor, coir or sisal matting is always a robust choice (although can be prone to staining) or look for outdoor rugs made from woven plastic that can be easily wiped or mopped.

Every craftsperson has moments when inspiration fails to strike. This is the time when your studio space can really provide the fillip you need to get going again. Whether you keep a tightly controlled bulletin board or cover every available wall space, the principle is the same – it's vital to surround yourself with images, words, sketches, swatches, keepsakes, photos and clippings that stimulate your work. Creative ideas rarely form in a vacuum. Inspiration boards can also bolster your mood – a witty quote or friendly photo can be a real tonic. If you have press cuttings from successful projects or images of work that you're proud of, get them pinned up. Positive feedback from clients, great reviews and kind words from other craftspeople can be a spur when you're having the inevitable periods of self-doubt that come with being creative.

SET UP CAMP You can't do craft properly if you have to keep packing up and moving spaces. Find a dedicated space that can house your tools, machinery and work-in-progress, whether it's a kiln, benchtop saw or finished pieces. Cadence Hays (opposite) has established herself in a corner, with benches and stools at just the right height for comfortable working.

CRAFT CORNER

Lise Meunier, ceramic artist, FRANCE

Hunting around fleamarkets is like prospecting for gold. Ceramic artist and stylist, Lise Meunier, has become adept at sieving her way through brocantes for precious pieces to smuggle back to her studio. It's a gorgeous space. Part studio, part home, it's a light, white apartment with large windows that open to the sky and a flower-filled balcony. 'Maybe one day I will put colour on the walls,' she muses. 'But white is neutral, enlarges the space and catches the light. And as the room is already full, I find white more visually relaxing.'

Around the studio, vintage pieces of furniture set the stage for her work – a large wooden canteen table and kitchen table provide ample work surfaces, while a small wardrobe 'bonnetière' and cooking cupboard keep her equipment in order. 'I also have lots of small drawers, lockers and doll furniture – very practical for storing small things. I also like using old boxes for storage – biscuit boxes, sewing boxes, tool boxes. There are toys, textiles, decorative items – it's an accumulation of objects of all kinds but they often have some connection to children and nature. These objects create the universe in my studio, give me inspiration and make me feel good.'

CREATIVE REINCARNATION Lise describes herself as someone who gives 'a second life to objects'. Her studio, a room off the main living space, is filled with toys, textiles and other decorative items, creating a 'personal universe' which informs her work. Most people would make it look like clutter; with Lise's expert eye, she makes it look like art.

TABLESCAPES Shiny new furniture just wouldn't fit with Lise's work or visual aesthetic; her studio is filled with old furniture, donated by friends, bought in brocantes or found on the street, including an old canteen trestle and a rustic kitchen table (overleaf).

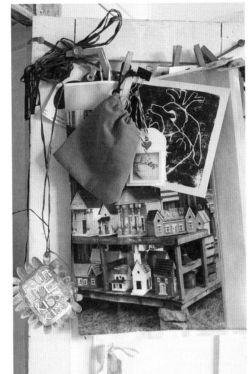

STUDIO INSIDE A STUDIO
Ariele Alasko, woodworker, US

An elegant simplicity defines Ariele Alasko's work and her studio. An artist who carves both spoons and other sculptural objects, her approach is satisfyingly timeless, especially when you consider that her studio isn't tucked away in a rural idyll, but nestling in the heart of a bustling, industrial New York neighbourhood. 'Practically everything I own is made from wood,' explains Ariele, 'so it's all browns and whites and blacks. I spend every day here, so it's homey and cosy while still being a dusty wood shop.'

Filled with junk-store furniture, street finds and lighting gathered on her yearly drives across the States, Ariele's studio combines the practicality of a workshop, a sharp design eye and a rural sensibility. Ariele even built a shingled loft for her office: 'It looks like a tree house nestled up in the corner of my workshop in the middle of this loud city.'

And when the tools are packed away and the dust has settled for the day, the studio has one more treat in store. 'I always dreamed of finding a corner studio with windows on two sides. I can see the sun set over the tip of Manhattan from one of the windows.' Now that's a room with a view.

WOOD IS GOOD It's perhaps only when you work closely with wood that you truly understand its inherent beauty as a decorative material. When you have a wonderful palette of muted shades at your fingertips – warm muddy browns, pale creamy whites and dark, rich chocolates – why spoil the look with man-made colours and garish patterns?

CREATIVE CONTRAST There's a delicious opposition between Ariele's rustic woodcarving and the hard, industrial backdrop of her studio. Conceptual contrasts – opposing themes such as nature/industrial or feminine/masculine – can create truly interesting studio aesthetics.

FASHION AND TEXTILES

FAR FROM BEING JUST A SEDATE FIRESIDE HABIT, MANY CREATIVE PROCESSES INVOLVING TEXTILES REQUIRE LOTS OF LEANING OVER WORKBENCHES OR LIFTING HEAVY ROLLS OF CLOTH. TIME TO GET SUPER-ORGANIZED OR YOU'LL FACE GETTING IN A TANGLE.

ABOVE LEFT: Ingrid Jansen's Dutch studio, Wood & Wool Stool, creates seating from crocheted wool and recycled wood. Her cubby-hole storage is the perfect way to keep yarn in order but also creates a colourful wall display above her work desk.

ABOVE CENTRE: Rolls of colourful bands and ribbons sit on shelves waiting to be chosen as the final flourish on one of Nick Fouquet's bespoke felt hats.

ABOVE RIGHT: A quiet corner in Helena Gavshon's textile studio, a building filled with reflected light, colour and pattern. White walls, desks and floors create a gallery-like backdrop for her beautiful fabric designs and archive material.

In terms of storage, textile crafts are amongst the most demanding – lots of small, intricate materials combined with plenty of sharp objects requires safe, logical storage. Magnetic knife racks, which you attach to the wall, are a good option for scissors, rotary cutters, eyelet pliers, stitch rippers, rulers and other metal hand tools. Bobbin holders are ideal for all your threads and can be mounted on the wall or hung from a pegboard.

Large fabric rolls (which can be incredibly heavy) are safest either stored upright, in bins or behind kickboards, or horizontal on industrial metal racking. Stack smaller bolts on open shelving, or in a deep glazed cupboard. Short lengths or 'drops' can be hung up on trouser hangers or rails or folded, while remnants for quilting and appliqué are best bundled and stored in clear containers. Clear jars and boxes are also ideal for haberdashery; there's nothing more satisfying than staring at rows of jars stuffed with brightly coloured buttons, ribbons and sequins.

For those of you who knit or crochet, you'll probably know that most wool is best stored in skeins or hanks rather than tight balls (this is because storing wool tightly bound can affect its elasticity); you only wind the yarn into a ball when you are ready to use it. Skeins also store more readily than balls, as they won't roll off a shelf, so open cubby holes and hanging storage are ideal. Open baskets, plastic bins, fabric wardrobe dividers and wire shoe racks are also popular choices if you want to be surrounded by your yarn in all its Technicolor glory.

SEW CREATIVE There are so many diverse skills that come under the umbrella of textiles – from the design process, to dyeing, printing and cutting lengths of fabric. Textile work can also be three-dimensional, from traditional upholstery to witty, dark-edged crochetdermy (opposite, below).

For sewing, bear in mind ergonomics and some general rules for comfortable working: when you use a sewing machine, your hands should be in a straight line with your wrists and forearms. For hand-sewing, your hands should be about 15cm (6 inches) above your elbows. Any chair should support your spine fully against the backrest and, when you are sitting down, your knees should be slightly lower than your hips. Bending over a cutting table can strain your back. To establish the perfect work surface height, stand with your elbows bent at right angles. Then, lower your hands just a fraction – this slightly obtuse angle is the right height for both your cutting table and ironing board, as it stops you banging your elbows. Kitchen countertop heights are a good guide. And, if you need a large, centralized cutting table, make sure you leave enough room to be able to manoeuvre around it comfortably. If you're stuck for space, look for foldable or drop-leaf tables. If your work involves plenty of measuring, take a tip from a haberdashers' shop and glue a long metal rule or a fabric tape measure along the edge or top of your work surface.

BOULEVARD WORKSHOP
Nick Fouquet, hatmaker, US

A while back, Nick Fouquet was wandering down LA's Venice Beach when he spied a cowboy wearing an old-fashioned Stetson. Nick asked him where he'd got it, and was surprised to discover that the cowboy had made the hat himself. That brief conversation proved to be a turning point and the start of a bespoke hatmaking business that now has a client list with more stars than the American flag. But starry Nick is not. With the work ethic of a craftsman and the down-to-earth vibe of someone unfazed by celebrity, he has created a craft space that's refreshingly unshowy and effortless in its rustic, bohemian style.

The studio is a practical space. Nick wanted to create artisan hats in a time-honoured way, but found that new tools and materials didn't fit his plan. So, ever resourceful, he set about acquiring vintage millinery equipment from retiring hatmakers across the States, and filled the workshop ready for production. And what a process it is. Hatmaking is hard work, it turns out. The raw material – beaver felt – has to be wrestled into form, steamed, pressed, sanded, stitched and then decorated, until the perfect result is achieved. Each hat is unique, reflecting the aesthetic and personality of the person using it. Bit like a studio really.

TRADITION REINVENTED Nick's workshop is filled with vintage millinery equipment such as mahogany block heads and industrial sewing machines, perfect for producing the kinds of hats for which he's become famous. But these aren't slavish copies of traditional headwear; Nick adds his own twists and flourishes to create a completely unique form, whether it's flame distressing the felt, applying paint splatters or adding a Fouquet poem handwritten on the band.

SHED STUDIO
Shauna Richardson, crochet artist, UK

What kind of studio do you need when you have so few tools that they could all be 'kept in a pencil case'? For crochet artist Shauna Richardson, the creation of a workshop at the end of her garden was less about space to work and more about space to retreat. 'I'm a bit of a hermit and a nest builder. As a child I spent my playtime in dens constructed out of cardboard boxes. Not much has altered in adult life, only now the den is made of bricks and mortar.'

An artist who has taken a timeless craft – crochet – and subverted it into an art form, Shauna's life-size animal sculptures turn taxidermy on its head with little more than a crochet hook and miles of mohair. 'My needs are small and I can work anywhere. The studio fulfils a more peaceful function.'

For Shauna, crocheting is instinctual; she could probably work blindfolded. The choice to have so much light was not so much an aid to work but more about a sense of well-being. Equally important is the inherent pleasure that comes with being outdoors and comfortable in all kinds of weather.

With so few material needs, Shauna hasn't had to angst over storage. A vast floor-to-ceiling bookcase accommodates her extensive collection of books and sketchbooks but apart from this, and a bespoke leather tool box, it's the animals that take centre stage. Not so much a studio, more a Noah's Ark.

BEST IN SHOW For crochetdermy artist Shauna Richardson, even the largest of her incredible animal creations are tooled with little more than a crochet hook and chunky yarn. Her menagerie of full-sized lions and trophy heads keep watch as Shauna works – sometimes sitting at a small desk, other times crouched on the floor – while light pours in through the glazed doors of her garden studio. Stairs lead up to valuable storage space for work in progress and admin.

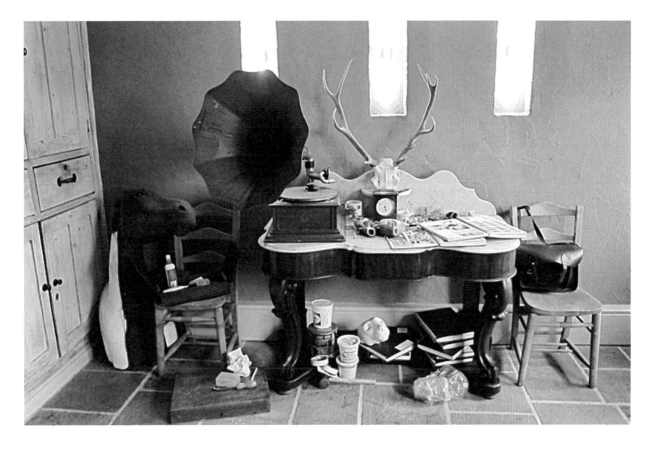

THREE STUDIOS IN ONE
Helena Gavshon, textile designer, UK

London can be a grey place at times. But you don't have to scratch the surface too deeply to find colour and pattern. On a quiet street, not far from the capital's famous Portobello Road, you'll find Helena Gavshon's textile studio. Running alongside the busy Paddington railway line and housed in an understated late 20th-century brick building, her workspace is a dazzling, kaleidoscopic jewel. Originally three separate units, Helena knocked through to create one huge studio with three distinct work areas. Each space has a mezzanine and is filled with natural light streaming in through industrial-style windows.

'Each room has a separate identity and purpose,' explains Helena, who has been at the helm of her own textile design company for more than two decades. 'I have a design studio in one space, a showroom for clients in another, and a library of antique reference books, albums and archives in the third studio.'

Helena is clearly passionate about pattern. At the heart of her success, and her work, is an understanding of the complex dialogue that goes on between vintage design and new, state-of-the-art ideas. 'I love making pattern, colour and texture work together,' she notes, 'Often the relationship isn't obvious and that's what's so exciting.' Her work consists of cutting-edge textile design, but her process often involves dipping into her studio's rich archive. Here you'll find antique and vintage garments, hand-painted wallpapers, swatch books and print inspiration sourced from across the world and spanning nearly 200 years of textile design.

A MARRIAGE OF STYLES Helena's approach to her studio space reflects her skill at blending old and cutting-edge design; there's a lovely interplay between the hard, industrial aesthetic of the building and the softening effect of layered colours, pattern and fabric.

MODERN RUSTIC Helen's large studio is also a space that embraces rustic, traditional elements – country tables, antique dressers, plan chests and heaving bookshelves – combined with contemporary accents, such as sleek white work desks and visible technology. A glorious array of fabric bridges the gap between the two styles – patterns that are traditional, timeless and resolutely cheerful.

FINE ART, ILLUSTRATION AND GRAPHIC DESIGN

THE WORD 'STUDIO' RESONATES WITH IMAGES OF SOMEONE DAUBING A CANVAS WITH EXUBERANT, BROAD STROKES. IT'S A CLICHÉ, AND FOR MOST ARTISTS AND ILLUSTRATORS, THE ONLY THING THAT REALLY MATTERS IS WORKING IN A SPACE THAT LETS YOU FOCUS AND BE INSPIRED.

ABOVE LEFT: If you live and breathe colour, and understand how it misbehaves under artificial light, an art studio bathed in diffuse sunshine comes top in your list of priorities.

ABOVE CENTRE: One of fine artist Sally Taylor's work surfaces. Above the desk she pins images and quotes, some from other artists, others self-generated, as both inspiration and motivation.

ABOVE RIGHT: Artist-illustrator Olaf Hajek keeps a sparse studio, elegant in its simplicity and the perfect foil for his often surreal, dream-like paintings.

Whether you're sculpting or sketching, working at a graphics laptop or creating collage, nothing is more important than access to good light. It matters in every creative practice, but particularly if you work with applied colour, as light has the power to radically affect what you see.

As home-owners, we love south-facing rooms (or north facing if you live in the southern hemisphere) as these provide plenty of sunshine. Not so good if you rely on constant, unchanging light for your work. Direct sunshine will cause the light in your studio to vary wildly, as the sun moves through the sky. It also creates hard shadows and strong highlights, bouncing off any light work surface and creating glare. If you need some level of control over the values, contrast and colour changes in your work, you'll need indirect light, which is softer and more consistent. Skylights are the ideal solution as they let in twice as much light as a vertical window, but we don't often have that much choice over the specification of a studio space. If you don't have north-facing windows, it's not a problem; covering the windows with tracing paper will diffuse the light nicely.

Natural light can also be supplemented with artificial light, which will even out any darker corners in the studio and allow you to work outside of daylight hours. Don't rely solely on incandescent bulbs as the light they give is too yellow, altering how cool colours appear. Daylight bulbs have improved dramatically in the past few years, so it's easy to pick up lamps, spots and easel clips that give you an even spread of perfect white light. Some artists enjoy mixing incandescent and daylight bulbs as the paintings they produce under these conditions don't tend to change too much under daylight or gallery spotlighting.

Desks and drawing surfaces all depend on the way you wish to work. If you paint, an easel is the obvious choice, but some people prefer to work on a horizontal surface such as the floor or a workbench, especially for collage and mixed media. Long periods of work at a desk will need a supportive chair and

SPACE TO WORK One minute your desk is a storage surface, the next it's an ideas forum, packed with a collage of thoughts and images. Fighting your way through clutter can frustrate the process, so try to give yourself room to spread and have some semblance of order, even if it's only at the beginning and end of a session.

worktable, but many artists find that they move around their studios, alternating between sitting and standing. A bar stool at a kitchen height worktop is often a comfortable solution for brief sessions, while an architect's/draughtsman's board and adjustable chair will provide a more ergonomic writing and close-drawing position, reducing the strain on your shoulders and back.

Most artists would agree that you should buy the best brushes you can afford. Bearing in mind that you can spend a fortune amassing a collection of good quality bristles, and they can last a lifetime if properly cared for, it's important you know how to clean and store them. How you do this depends on the kind of paint you're using. To clean a watercolour brush you need to wipe it first with a lint free cloth and then wash it using mild liquid soap and cool water. Very strong soap can strip the natural oils from the bristles and hot water may cause any watercolour paint left on the brush to harden. If you've been working with oils, again wipe the excess paint off with a rag and then wash the brush in a jar of brush cleaner. Once most of the colour has been removed you can finish with a final wash using mild liquid soap and warm water. With both watercolour and

oil brushes, dry them off with a paper towel, reshape the brush head with your fingers and then store upright in a jar. If you're not planning to use them for a while, pop them in a dry, sealed box to keep the moths away. It's also worth saying that, if you use both watercolours and oils, keep your brushes separate and don't use the same brush for both mediums.

If you're using solvents to thin paint or clean brushes, you'll need to make provision for safe storage and removal. It might sound over-cautious, but solvents are both poisonous and flammable so it's prudent to keep them properly labelled and locked away in a metal storage cabinet. Spirit-soaked rags are also a fire hazard, so don't be tempted to throw them in your normal waste paper basket: you'll need a galvanized steel bin with a lid. Pour used solvents into a non-flammable container, and despose of it at your local recycling centre.

If your work is predominately digital, this should be the starting point when it comes to thinking about your studio. Buy the best kit you can afford and think about whether you'll need to work from more than one screen, or a combination of a computer and laptop/tablet. Do you need a separate keyboard? Where's the printer or scanner going to sit? All of this will then dictate the size and arrangement of your work desk.

The designers' maxim is often cheap desk, pricey chair; you'll be sitting for hours so it's vital to keep your back happy. If your only option is a tired old office chair on castors, take heart; they are relatively easy to re-cover. The fabric seat pads are often held in place by bolts and screws; once undone you then pop the seat pad out of its plastic casing and then staple new fabric around the pad.

In terms of location, industrial loft studios are a nice idea and the quality of natural light is often unbeatable, but for a job where you are sitting for protracted periods of time, old manufacturing buildings can be cold, draughty and expensive to heat. A warm, dry office or spare room will be just dandy, as long as you've got plenty of natural light and strategic task lighting (overhead strip lights are not only spirit-sapping but have been linked to migraines and low levels of the hormone melatonin, which controls the body clock).

Provision for listening to music is worth considering. One of the joys of creative work is that you can often work and listen simultaneously. It all depends on the task in hand. Studies have shown that moderate noise levels can improve the creative process, but that loud noises or lyrics can make it tricky to concentrate if you're doing any language-related tasks (like reading reference material or writing). Low-immersion or visual tasks, such as drawing or doing something repetitive, on the other hand can benefit from background music.

Of all of the working environments, the graphic design studio comes closest to what we think of as the traditional 'office', but that doesn't mean aesthetics don't matter. Designers and illustrators are as sensitive to their surroundings as a fine artist, so it's important the space reflects and bolsters your creative aspirations. It also needs to feel cosy and comfortable. Art, reference books, pinboards, vintage posters, huge chalkboards, a bright sofa, colouring-in walls, quirky feature lighting, kettle, favourite mug and biscuits – it's essentially all about creating an environment that you want to spend time in.

SETTLE IN Fundamentally, a studio needs to be a space that you want to spend quality time in. Whether it's a feeling of being at home, a creative rush or just a sense of calm you need, try to establish the right mood through decor, personal objects, tools of your trade and inspiring materials, as in this artists's studio in a Scandinavian summerhouse (opposite).

STONE BARN STUDIO
Sally Taylor, fine artist, UK

In a stone barn in the Yorkshire countryside, Sally Taylor is kneeling on gloss-grey floorboards, sorting through found papers and old text books. Sally, whose drawings and collages focus on the human head and mouth, has created a studio that not only reflects her art but also actively helps keep her grounded and focused. The space, like Sally's work, is brilliant white – a gloriously plain background onto which she's layered simple, bright pieces of furniture and hundreds of drawings and mementos. 'The studio is like my artwork,' Sally explains, 'white and bright with tiny flecks of colours. It's cold and rustic, but I need that sense of hardship – it reflects the struggle in my work. I can't imagine making my work in a clean, new space.'

For all the building's challenges, Sally has created a studio full of warmth and meaning. A large, red sofa provides a place for thinking and looking, a vital part of any art practice. Simple IKEA shelves and salvaged school furniture reflect Sally's aesthetic at home and her love of unshowy decor and simple forms. She's also a fan of neon pops of colour, whether it's an acid yellow bookshelf or her choice of cardigan: 'They're not easy shades, you can't help but have an emotional reaction to them.' Around the interior the walls are also covered with source material – postcards, cut-outs, sketches and hand-scribbled messages – things that keep Sally motivated. A folder, attached to the wall, contains scraps of paper with the nice things that people have said about her work; with four nominations for the Jerwood Drawing Prize and an appearance at the Venice Biennale under her belt, you wonder whether she really needs it.

ART ON THE FARM Occupying such a rough space keeps Sally focused and driven, but it also has its practical advantages. The old stone walls and make-shift partitions are the ideal low-tech surface for the endless sticking and re-sticking of Sally's work and scribbled mottos. The walls and a portion of the roof are simply whitewashed, brightening the space and keeping stone dust at bay, while the floor has its bi-annual coat of gloss grey, a light but practical colour.

CONVERTED GARAGE STUDIO

Lisa Congdon, artist, US

They say that practice makes perfect. Twelve years of being an artist and three studios down, it's only now Lisa Congdon has a space that meets all her needs. Using all the knowledge she gleaned from her expereince in her previous workspaces, she's carved out a studio that's not only deeply practical, but also happens to be really rather gorgeous.

The space was originally a detached garage. Lisa gutted the interior and started again, insulating, dry walling and adding extra windows to let natural light flood in. 'I then spent some time in the space thinking about all my typical studio needs,' she explains. 'Space to draw and paint, shelves for books, storage for packing and shipping supplies, a standing desk for packing and shipping my online orders and a built-in desk area.' A full-width pegboard keeps all Lisa's tools and tapes in order, while under the desk white plastic stacking boxes and laundry drawers blend into the background, leaving Lisa's work to shine.

LIGHT FANTASTIC Ever the pragmatist, Lisa Congdon has transformed an unpromising detached garage in the grounds of her home into a buzzing, effective workspace. She's divided the studio into zones, distinct areas with specific functions. For her drawing and painting work, Lisa needs as much natural light as possible. This space – right in front of the glazed garage doors and entrance – is ideal and the perfect spot for a simple trestle table and stool.

With so many facets to her creative life – author, painter and illustrator – a messy studio wasn't an option. 'I like to keep things orderly – that helps me be creative because I'm not distracted by disorganization. I can work on a painting and while it's drying hop over and get on the computer to catch up on email.'

It's a refreshingly organized approach and one that even translates into her choice of decor. Colour is everywhere, but it's carefully controlled. White, the great calmer of spaces, reins in the excesses. 'I work in a lot of colour and I also own a lot of colourful things – collections, books, ephemera. I thought they would look great against an all-white background. It looks fresh and modern and all of my colourful things really pop.'

ORDER REIGNS SUPREME Another distinct zone in Lisa's studio is her built-in desk area, where she can catch up on emails and paperwork without any creative distractions. Above the desk, Lisa's open storage shelves allow her to be inspired by her colourful collections and favourite books without clutter compromising her work. Lisa's standing desk for packing and shipping her work to clients (overleaf) is equally well thought out.

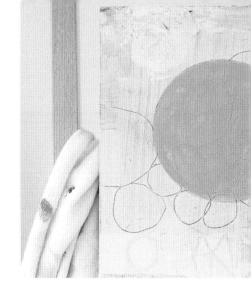

LIVE–WORK SPACE
Mari Andrews, artist and sculptor, US

There are plenty of things to covet about Mari Andrews' work space. For a start, it's light. Really light. Two enormous skylights and a wall of south-facing windows flood her white-walled studio. It's also dazzlingly vast. 'My favourite detail is a window, up in the living area,' she explains. 'I have a second floor where I can look down in the studio and get a completely different perspective on my work.'

Around the ground floor space are hundreds of glass jars, filled with seeds, bark and the other natural objets trouvés that form the basis of Mari's work. Part sweet shop, part biology lab, it's beautifully ordered thanks to rows and rows of salvaged shelves: 'The studio is chock full of materials I've pick up on my travels. I've also made space for wires, string, adhesives, pigments, paper, mediums, a welder and a drill press, as well as all my hand tools.'

A wheeled worktable, door and sawhorses, and a table in the middle of the room provide ample and flexible work surfaces for Mari's different processes. 'I often have several things going on at once, with works drying, flattening, joining or just experimenting with materials. Being able to move around the table is very important.' And does the space work? 'I absolutely love my studio!' she laughs. 'I came from a very large family of ten children and never had my own bedroom. This is better than having my own bedroom – it is my place of work, play, experimentation, contemplation, struggle and joy.'

ALL IN ONE Mari Andrews' studio is vast. But it needs to be. Not only does she create here, she lives here too. With 6-m (20-foot) high ceilings, the studio also accommodates a second floor that houses a kitchen, dining room, living room and bedroom. This leaves the whole ground floor free to be a workspace-cum-laboratory.

STREET-FRONT STUDIO

Olaf Hajek, illustrator, GERMANY

'You find magic wherever you look. Sit back and relax, all you need is a book.' Children's author Dr Seuss clearly understood the power of books to expand the imagination and trigger creativity. It's a quality Berlin-based artist and illustrator, Olaf Hajek, also draws on in his fantastical, surreal, deliciously colourful work.

'Books are an amazing source of inspiration,' he explains. 'Today I can Google everything, but there is nothing more inspirational than a beautiful book. I love spending time in art book stores and try to find precious treasures, such as books about botanical illustrations, Indian miniatures or African patterns; all elements which will find their way into my work.'

It's no surprise, then, that books are a key part of Olaf's studio. Housed in a simple wooden bookcase, designed by Olaf and built by a local carpenter, this wonderful archive shares space with pots of paint, quirky figures and favourite finds. Beyond the books, it's a simple space – practical in its lack of clutter, elegant in its limited choice of furniture and decor. Dotted around the studio are also Danish chairs and a simple wooden stool. These, and an iconic Eiermann desk, provide everything Olaf needs to sit and create, whether it's his latest illustration for fashion brand Hermès or a spread for *New York Times* magazine.

OPEN FOR BUSINESS On the ground floor of a quiet street in the middle of buzzing Berlin Mitte, sits a very content Olaf Hajek. 'I love to open up the door in the morning, open the shutters and make my first coffee … it's like a second home.' A simple concrete floor, white walls and pared-back furniture create the ideal neutral background for Olaf's vibrant work, books and art materials.

WRITING, BLOGGING AND PHOTOGRAPHY

WHETHER YOU WRITE FOR A LIVING, TAKE PHOTOGRAPHS OR DO A COMBINATION OF THE TWO, THERE'S NOTHING LIKE A DEDICATED WORKSPACE TO HELP YOU FIND FOCUS AND FLOW.

ABOVE LEFT: Agata Dimmich's Italian garden studio is the perfect retreat where she can write her blog 'Passion Shake' and find that all important creative solace.

ABOVE CENTRE: Set designers and art directors Lord Whitney find a blank corner in their industrial-sized studio to set up a photography space.

ABOVE RIGHT: Fashion entrepreneurs Sarah Vickers and Kiel James Patrick share a double desk, perfect for blogging about their latest campaign or editing copy.

What does a writer really need? Beyond the basics – a laptop or a pen and pad – writing is a wonderfully mobile skill. You find authors like to write in different places – one minute you're scribbling away in a favourite armchair, the next head-down at a busy cafe table. A new environment can clear a moment of writer's block, offering a fresh perspective and a way forward, but there comes a point when you need a proper, dedicated space. If you write for a living and need to spend days, not just hours, sitting hunched over a manuscript, a proper desk (however small) and comfy chair are non-negotiable. Warmth and quiet are also pre-requisites – you simply can't concentrate if the room is too cold or noisy.

Create a routine or ambience that triggers your writing to flow – click on a reading lamp, light a candle, make a hot drink. There's a temptation to shove your desk up in a corner and work with your back to the room, but it can be bleak to spend an entire day staring at a blank wall. If that's happening, try turning your desk to face into the room. Failing that, when you look up from your desk make sure there's something to see – a much-loved painting or photograph, a window with a view, a mirror or a shelf filled with favourite things.

Books are friends. They not only provide a source of inspiration, but their presence is comforting. If you're a published author it's also a bit of thrill to be surrounded by copies of your own books – when moments of doubt or brain-death strike, being reminded that you have written and can write are incredibly soothing. Most journalists, bloggers and authors don't just rely on the typed word – the process of writing with a pen is very different from typing, it unlocks different thoughts and ways of working. Notebooks are essential and should be kept safely and logically stored – yesterday's germ of an idea can be tomorrow's bestseller. Treat yourself to some good pens and pencils.

And when inspiration has deserted you, the worst thing you can do is sit and stare at your computer. Writing is a peculiar task – it doesn't respond well to pressure – so the key is to do something that either forces your brain to think in a different way, or to get out of the studio environment altogether. Stop writing and stop trying. Go and do something practical – make a meal, paint a wall, vacuum the hallway – anything that doesn't involve overthinking and exercises a different part of your brain. Better still, get outside. Go for a coffee, take the dog for a walk, do some weeding. Escape the monastic silence of writing – gossip with a friend, watch or listen to something that makes you laugh. And then, when you feel ready to try again, remind yourself it doesn't have to be perfect.

CREATIVE CONDITIONS If you've ever suffered from writer's block, you'll know important routine and surroundings are to your work, whether it's giving your writing equipment its own special place, like stylist Katrin Bååth (above left), or finding a corner that gives you peace and perspective, like Ilaria Chiaratti Bonomi's blogging studio (opposite).

LESS IS MORE For photographer Julia Bostock, access to light and clear space are vital (below). No two shoot days are exactly the same, so she created a studio with large windows, minimalist decor and moveable furniture.

FLEXIBLE FRIEND Holly Becker's German home studio needs to adapt to different tasks, depending on the project. A large worktable is the ideal solution, perfect for team meetings one minute, and setting up product photography the next (opposite).

When it comes to snapping images, you could write an entire book on how to set up a photographic studio. And much of the advice will vary depending on what you're shooting. Bloggers, for example, have got small-scale studios down to a fine art, creating great shots with little more than a tripod, tabletop, flash and a window. In this instance, a 'studio' can be created in almost any corner of your home and with the help of a few different backgrounds and a bounce card, you can take some very convincing tight shots of products and craft projects.

For these small-scale shoots, the window will be your main source of light and your shooting surface needs to be positioned so the light hits your subject side on (sidelight almost always looks better than shooting directly into the light or with the light behind you). Bright sunlight will also create harsh shadows and glare, so tissue paper or white gauze at the window will diffuse any direct light. If you've got a choice, pick the largest window – the bigger the window, the softer and less focused the light.

For work surfaces, don't invest in anything too static or heavy. Trestle legs and a sheet of timber or a foldaway table are good choices as you may find yourself constantly adjusting your shooting surface to capture the best light. Better still, you can move your table to one side entirely and use the floor space for top shots without too much effort. To create seamless backgrounds, wide rolls of white paper are ideal, but you can also use large sheets of card or foamboard. In such a small space and with expensive equipment at work, sensible storage is a must. Open shelves are ideal for holding everything from props to backgrounds, styling tools, reference books, clamps, tapes, printers and photographic kit. And, while most of your images will be stored digitally, there's something to be said for pinning up a large selection of your favourite work on your studio walls. It's not only a boost to be surrounded by inspiring images, but it can also help your practice – comparing images, looking at them in different lights, musing over their composition; it all helps you improve your technique and eye.

Larger work, unsurprisingly, requires a large studio. Photography students are always told to leave 'room to zoom', as wide-angle lenses will distort whatever you are trying to capture. As a general rule, if you are trying to photograph a person standing, for example, you need to leave at least 6m (19 feet) between your backdrop and lens. Low ceilings can create lighting issues, bouncing too much light back into the room and getting in the way of everything from light stands to booms – so ceiling heights of 4m (13 feet) are a minimum if you're doing any kind of fashion or full portrait photography. With those kinds of room size requirements, it's clear to see why so many professional photographers create high-ceilinged studios from scratch or use commercial or industrial premises.

SHARED WORKSPACE
Kiel James Patrick & Sarah Vickers, bloggers, US

When the American industrialist Henry Ford famously said 'Coming together is a beginning; keeping together is progress; working together is success,' he could have as easily been talking about marriage as manufacturing. Young husband and wife team Kiel James Patrick and Sarah Vickers are fashion entrepreneurs and social media giants, a feat that requires patience, commitment and, above all, a workspace that allows them to flourish. 'There are times when we love working side by side on projects,' explains Sarah, 'and others when we need our own space. It was important for Kiel and I to have a space that would serve as a continuous source of inspiration combined with the comforts of home.'

But creating a workspace that suits two people is easier said than done, especially when aesthetics matter. 'It is a mix of both of our personalities. When

WORKING SIDE BY SIDE Compromise doesn't have to be a dirty word. For fashion designers and social media giants Sarah Vickers and Kiel James Patrick, the coming together of their collective taste has resulted in something quite splendid: a shared workspace – nicknamed Fort Cochicawick – that's stuffed with character. Here, taxidermy and club seating rub shoulders with Persian rugs and pretty accents.

ALEXA CHUNG

we were deciding on a colour we searched high and low for the perfect shade of green to bring the room together. My tastes lean towards girly and whimsical while Kiel loves all things adventure and nautical.'

The solution was to create an office that allowed Keil and Sarah the flexibility to work closely or in creative solitude: 'We each have sections of the office that are our own. I had to have a daybed by the window with floral cushions and plenty of natural light. Kiel needed a secret loft within the office that he named Fort Firebird. There is a ladder above the stairs to get to it and it also has a daybed and extra light if he's looking for a quiet place to work without interruption.'

LOVE WHAT YOU SEE Keen to have all their books, antiques, magazines and mementos on display, Kiel and Sarah have made sure there's not a single section of the office that doesn't serve as storage or inspiration. Generous seating and witty accents keep the space feeling young and relaxed.

CREATIVE HOME OFFICE

Holly Becker, photographer, stylist & blogger, GERMANY

When you're a busy blogger you need a studio that not only inspires what you do but also helps you stay focused. In Holly Becker's light, bright Hanover apartment, her dedicated workspace is a masterclass in how to stay creative and productive. 'I like to start each day on a blank canvas,' she explains. 'If my workspace is full of colour, pattern and clutter I cannot accomplish nearly as much. When I leave my office cluttered for a few days, because I get too busy on a project, I notice my work is negatively impacted. I cannot think as clearly.'

The solution? To keep clutter tightly controlled and create a space with plenty of clever storage. At the heart of the workspace sits a large white wooden cupboard, the perfect hiding place for Holly's 'ingredients', 'fabric, washi tape, tissue paper, scissors, glitter, beads, props, everything you can imagine – it's in there! I like my storage to be in the room but not obvious; once it's closed, you have no idea of what is tucked away inside.' Creating the right 'mood' for work is also vital, especially if you need to concentrate. For Holly, candles and fresh flowers help her stay focused; 'I feel better when the room smells nice and there is a certain mood about the space. I also earn more in return when I am productive, so I see it as a double win!'

PERFECT ORDER In any given week, Holly Becker can be writing, photographing, making and designing, so it's vital her workspace can multi-task. Simple, beautifully designed pieces, such as her Danish wooden table, and a light wall palette provide the backbone of the space, leaving Holly the freedom to add softening accents such as fresh flowers, candles and textural fabrics.

REMODELLED STUDIO
Julia Bostock, photographer, UK

Julia Bostock's approach is playful and irreverent, perfect for shooting children's fashion. A creative urge to bend the rules is also evident in her studio, a space she's transformed from an old barn and cottage deep in the Suffolk countryside.

Many people would have felt constricted by the limitations of old buildings, but Julia's vision was clear from the start. 'It was fun to get involved right from the beginning – it evolved with our architect friend who suggested joining the barn and cottage together by covering the yard and creating one big space.'

Natural light was the priority. Away came the first-floor ceiling, opening up the barn from floor to raftered roof, followed by punching a huge picture window through the outside wall. Julia's eye for contemporary building materials – shuttered concrete, poured resin and glulam beams – gives the studio an edge, softened by salvaged wooden floors, exposed brick and reclaimed furniture.

Julia's motivation is everywhere. 'My board is my inspiration,' she explains. 'I pin everything from a snip of fluoro orange ribbon to a postcard from Brazil with some beautiful type. My shelves above my computer are important to remind me of what's outside my bubble.'

Work surfaces are large and numerous. 'I have lots of tables – old and new – for laying out work, editing photographs, team meetings and communal lunches. The space has also seen lots of great parties, so it has a really happy feel.'

SPACE FOR INSPIRATION In the corner of an otherwise minimalist studio, Julia has created a desk space that's surrounded with images, snippets and little paintings. They provide her with a reminder of places she's been or dreams about visiting, as well as linking Julia to the things outside her work life.

OLD BUILDING NEW STUDIO It takes someone with real artistic
vision to transform a tired old barn into such a dynamic workspace.
Edgy design materials, such as shuttered concrete, set a modern tone
which is then tempered with Julia's clever use of softer, natural accents
such as reclaimed wood, leather and cow-hide.

WORKSHOPS AND UPCYCLING

OF ALL STUDIO SPACES, A WORKSHOP IS THE ONE THAT NEEDS TO START WITH THE VERY BASICS. MOST WORKBENCH ACTIVITIES INVOLVE POWER TOOLS, HEAVY EQUIPMENT AND HAZARDOUS SUBSTANCES, SO IT'S IMPORTANT YOUR SPACE IS SAFE BEFORE ANY OTHER CONSIDERATION.

ABOVE LEFT: Upcycling expert Charis Williams' robust workshop was built out of unwanted materials, including scrap timber and electric fittings reclaimed from a building site skip.

ABOVE CENTRE: Nicolas Flachot's industrial workspace, with its old factory furniture and enamel lights, provides an ideal backdrop for his reclaimed letters and fonts.

ABOVE RIGHT: In Max McMurdo's recycling workshop he takes everyday landfill and upcycles them into witty, functional and often beautiful pieces of furniture and accessories.

Workshop safety is partly about practicalities but also about practice – get your health and safety head on and work with all the common dangers in mind: it's not an exhaustive list but things such as poor ventilation, cluttered workbenches, chemicals in unmarked containers, trailing wires, messy floors, inadequate lighting, top-heavy shelving and missing machinery guards are accidents waiting to happen.

If you have any control over the layout of your workshop, plan it on paper first and ask yourself the question, 'What's going to happen when?' At the very least, your workshop needs to be organized so that your most often-used tools are easily accessible and there's plenty of room to manoeuvre any materials you might be handling. Large sheet materials and long lengths of timber and metal can be especially tricky to accommodate.

Some pieces of kit will need their own dedicated power circuits, for example, or specialist ventilation. When it comes to planning the electrics, always put in more outlets and lighting points than you think you need. If you are converting a shed or garage into a workshop, ask your electrician to wire your lighting circuit separately from your sockets (outlets) – that way, if a power tool trips the electrics you're not left scrabbling around in the dark. Ventilation is important, too. Sawdust, paints, varnishes, solvents and glues can all be lethal, so it's vital you install some kind of dust and fume extraction (you may also need your workshop to be dust-free when you're applying a finish).

Your workbench will be the lynchpin of your studio so choose one that's large, heavy and will take a thorough pounding. A normal table just won't be up to the job – a workbench needs to be solid, so it can resist the forces being placed against it, and robust enough so it doesn't shake itself to pieces with every push of a hand saw or knock of a hammer. If you're designing a workbench from scratch remember that you can't build a bench that fulfils every function – there's always some compromise – but you can predict which types of work you'll do most often and how you'll want to work around the bench. For instance, do you need access from all sides, or can it go against a wall? Do you need to permanently mount machinery or vices? If space is limited, could your workbench have wheels or would this make sawing and planing awkward? Serious woodworkers swear by Scott Landis' *The Workbench Book*, but if in doubt, keep it simple.

ORGANIZATION When it comes to organizing your workshop, start from the basic premise that you need to keep your most-often-used tools nearby, and have enough floor and bench space to handle your materials and work safely. Rook's Books binding tools and letter stamps (above left) are neatly shelved, while Blok Knives have created different areas of work surfaces for different stages of production (opposite).

Lighting is critical to both safe and effective working. Don't rely on one source. Combine generous overhead lighting (which will provide a consistent spread of light over your workshop) with task lighting. Spotlights are ideal for the latter and can be placed over workbenches, machinery and storage areas to help you work accurately. When you are thinking about where to position task lights, it's worth experimenting to see whether certain positions create shadows over the very area you are attempting to illuminate. And don't forget to make the most of any natural light – painting your workshop white will bounce any daylight around and add to the mix.

When it comes to storage, there are lots of robust solutions. Pegboards are excellent for vertical storage and you can buy so many different accessories – hooks, shelves, baskets, clips, spools and so on – that there's an almost inexhaustible way to keep things safely stowed. Pegboards are also endlessly adaptable – nothing is permanently fixed so you can change your storage needs to suit. Component drawers are handy for fiddly materials and a staple of most well-organized workshops; the handful of nails in a jam jar approach to storage is just too crude for most workshops, where small items such as screws, nuts and nails are size-specific and need to be kept separate.

Wheeled storage boxes and drawers on castors are also useful if you work in various areas of the workshop but don't want your tools in one place. If you have an open ceiling in your workshop, make the most of its storage potential – long lengths of materials such as metal or timber can be kept safely stowed in the rafters above your head. Heavy-duty metal wall cabinets are ideal for chemicals, paints and solvents – anything that needs to be locked away from heat sources and out of harms' way. Magnetic strips are also really handy for small tools – spanners, scoring knives, pliers, wire strippers – and stop you having to rifle around in a hurry. It sounds obvious, but how you use your tools will also affect the productivity of your workspace – putting things away after you've used them, keeping tools sharp and clean, and clearing away wood shavings and debris will all improve the experience of being in your workshop.

Most workshop floors are concrete or timber. Timber is a sound option, soft on the acoustics and with a few coats of varnish, fairly robust. It doesn't like being constantly bashed or soaked in chemicals or oils, however, so if your creative ventures are fairly industrial, concrete's a better option. Unfinished concrete can be a bit powdery and porous, but a few coats of garage floor sealant or concrete paint will give you a durable, tough finish.

UPCYCLER'S UTOPIA Robust reclaimed shelves, generous workbenches and plenty of plug sockets (outlets) epitomize Max McMurdo's deeply pragmatic approach to his upcycling workshop, where he transforms potential landfill into desirable pieces of design (opposite).

WELL LIT Good lighting is key to a safe and productive workshop, especially task lighting for using tools and cutting materials. But it can also be beautiful, such as Heather Ross's simple bayonet tripod light (below).

SIMPLE, BRIGHT STUDIO
Nicolas Flachot, recycled signage designer, FRANCE

In a cobbled courtyard, off the Rue Saint-Denis in Paris, you'll find an old textile workshop. It's a vast, light-filled space with huge expanses of glass, stark walls and bare floors, and the perfect backdrop for one of the most incredible collections of vintage signs you'll ever hope to see. Industrial shelves groan with letters from the alphabet, enamel factory lights illuminate a workbench filled with words, and every inch of wall space glows with fantastic fonts waiting to find a new home. This is Kidimo, a workshop, treasure trove and showroom all in one. It's the brain child of self-confessed fleamarket junkie Nicolas Flachot, a man who takes old, unwanted lettering from restaurants, factories and other redundant businesses and upcycles them into personalized logos, pithy phrases and words of art. From American number plates to retro supermarket signs, blousy fairground lettering to Art Nouveau flourishes, he sees beauty and poetry in typography, whatever its form.

What started as a search to find three vintage letters to spell his daughter's name – LOU – has turned into a glorious obsession and healthy interiors business. This huge workshop is now home to numbers, fonts and signs, of all shapes, sizes and materials. Customers pop in with their quirky requests – a huge 'S' for a friend's birthday, the word 'Cuisine' to decorate a kitchen, or a huge 'Grrrrr!' just for the hell of it. Anything is possible, it seems. Just say the word.

FROM FABRIC TO FONTS Nicolas Flachot's workshop was, in a previous life, a textile factory. The Sentier district, where his studio is located, was once the beating heart of Paris' clothing industry. It's still a textile area, but times are changing fast and many of the now redundant loft-like spaces are being snapped up by artists, craftspeople and internet businesses. All the things that made it a great space for textiles – large open rooms, lots of natural light and robust industrial fittings – make it ideal for its new incarnation as a font workshop.

EASY AS ABC With thousands of vintage letters, stars and other shapes in stock, it would be easy for the Kidimo studio to feel like a scrap yard. Nicolas' use of simple industrial accents and white walls, however, gives the space a gallery-like feel and allows the fonts the opportunity to be shown off.

UPCYCLED WORKSHOP
Charis Williams, upcycler, UK

Whenever 'Salvage Sister' Charis Williams has a bad day, she looks at her self-built studio and tells herself 'I built this, I can do anything.' No mean feat when you realize that she did it unaided, using free, unwanted materials and with no previous building experience under her belt. 'I built my workshop because I had to have somewhere to work,' she explains. 'I do a lot of upcycling, designing and making with salvaged materials and, until I built the workshop, everything was being created in my kitchen and dining room.'

Practical and pragmatic, Charis began the process by hunting for materials. 'I knew I wanted to use pallets for the frame as they are robust, weatherproof and best of all can be found anywhere for free.' She damp-proofed the workshop using unwanted vinyl advertising banners and finished by cladding the building with boards sourced from a free-cycling website. There can't be many better ways to demonstrate the potential of upcycling. 'I used the build to show people the massive amounts of usable materials that are needlessly sent to landfill every day. My business is creating beautiful and useful items from "trash" so it's the perfect place for me to work; it also serves as an inspiration to me every day.'

BUILD IT YOURSELF Charis built her workshop from unwanted materials that she found for free around Brighton. From discarded pallets to salvaged patio slabs, reclaimed fence posts to rolls of advertising banners, she crafted a space from trash and turned landfill into valuable workshop space. The old wingback that sits in her workshop was found abandoned on the pavement and comes in handy as a coffee break chair or a place to sit and paint.

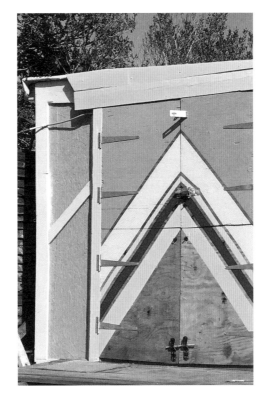

PART THREE
STUDIO ELEMENTS

PLANNING
YOUR STUDIO

A studio is essentially a means to an end and its principal virtue should be that it doesn't impede your work. Better still if it can actively make it easier. With that in mind, it's important to get all the practical details planned out before the fun really starts. Here's a quick checklist to run through if you're sizing up a room or planning to convert a space into a studio:

ACCESS – Do you have specific needs? Stairs, narrow doorways, corridors and other space restrictions can affect whether you, visitors, equipment and large materials can move freely through the space.

SPACE – What floor area and ceiling height do you really need to operate effectively and safely? Imagine all your furniture and equipment in the space. Are there safe working areas around tables and machinery? Do you need to be able to view your work from a distance?

SERVICES – Think about whether you need running water and a working sink. What about toilet, food preparation and washing facilities? Where will any waste water go?

ELECTRICITY – Establish how your studio is supplied. If you share a space is it metered? Is there a fuse box or RCD protection? Kilns, ovens and large machinery may need more substantial supplies – check with an electrician.

HEATING & VENTILATION – How is the space kept warm and can you afford to run it? Look for signs of insulation. If you are working with solvents or dust, is there proper ventilation?

LIGHTING – Few studios come with adequate lighting. Quick DIY fixes include LED ceiling tracks, clip-on spotlights and adjustable table work lamps, all of which can be plugged into existing sockets (outlets).

CONNOISSEURS OF MAKE-BELIEVE Amy Lord and Rebekah Whitney needed a space that could house their larger-than-life set design and art direction business 'Lord Whitney' (right and previous page). With a huge amount of vision, they transformed the top floor of an old leather mill into a creative hub filled with props, studio equipment and cleverly defined work areas.

GETTING
ORGANIZED

There are similarities between designing a kitchen and planning a studio; of all our living spaces, studios and kitchens are the busiest and most productive and, as such, require careful organization. Critical elements such as work surfaces, storage and lighting need proper consideration and, more importantly, an understanding of how you move between the various areas of your studio.

Think about the 'flow' of your studio on a typical day. Is there a particular way you always work? If you start a project, are there distinct making stages? Do you need to keep materials separate from the work area? Do you need clear access between two work surfaces or a table and a sink, for example? The easiest way to tackle this is to draw a small-scale plan of your space and then cut out paper templates of all your studio basics – worktable, sink, machinery, storage cupboard, drying space etc. Play around with the layout, remembering to give yourself plenty of room to manoeuvre. If you've got a large studio space, however, resist the urge to push everything to the walls – you could end up walking miles. Draw any electrical sockets (outlets), lights and plumbing on your plan. Go over the top with storage – aim to keep most things safely stowed away on shelves, hung from walls or tucked in cupboards. Use dead spaces such as under stairs, above desks and machinery, or in the rafters.

And, if you're stuck for ideas, don't reinvent the wheel – go and see how someone else has done it. Most areas have 'open studio' days, where you can wander around workshops and studios, chatting to artists and getting inspired. Visit people from all disciplines – cross fertilize and find out how different artists and craftspeople solve the same studio problems.

WEAVING OLD AND NEW If you work with found threads and scraps of vintage textiles, coherent storage is a must. Textile artist Penny Leaver Green has brilliantly combined period drawers and glass-fronted cupboards with contemporary acrylic boxes from Habitat. Artists are often adept at creating beautiful spaces on modest budgets. Penny's clever use of a white-painted backdrop, antique furniture and display storage creates a studio packed with character and warmth.

CREATIVE HUB Canadian artist, photographer and stylist Heather Ross created a dream workspace with a nature-inspired aesthetic. Designed to be a portable studio, she put together a foldable, stackable, rolling space complete with a twine-and-peg hanging system for her book proofs.

STUDIO PRACTICE

You can only be a creative person if you create. But setting out on an artistic or craft endeavour can be a bit intimidating. What if my work isn't any good? What if no one else likes it? What if I can't finish things in the time I've allowed myself? Good studio practice is all about setting yourself some rules and creating a working pattern that helps keep you inspired, motivated and focused. There are a million ways to be creative, but only a handful of universal truths that will always keep you on your journey:

COMMIT TO PRACTICE
Studio practice is just that . . . practice. So often we focus on the finished painting or the perfectly fired pot, but the process is just as important as the end result. Studio practice is loosely analogous with sports practice – the more you do, the better you get, the more likely you are to be happy with the end result. The process is also the important bit, because it's where you discover new things about yourself and your work.

EXPERIMENT & KEEP LEARNING
Once you stop trying new things your work can become stale and mannered. It's vital to not only hone your existing skills, but also attempt new ones. Go on courses. Read up on new techniques. Visit other artists or craftspeople. Take risks. Don't believe anyone who says 'You can't teach an old dog new tricks.'

KNOW YOURSELF
We're our own worst critics. Sometimes it's the fault-finding inner voice – 'I'm not good enough' – but often it's those self-defeating practices that will really trip you up. Being easily distracted, finding other chores to do first, getting to the studio late – all great ways to sabotage your work. Know you are doing it and find strategies that are tailored for you – if you are constantly checking your phone, for example, don't bring it into the studio. Set clear, achievable goals for the day and reward yourself for reaching them.

BE COMFORTABLE
A true artist should suffer, right? Bah. Discomfort is distracting, whether it's a freezing cold studio or the wrong pair of shoes. Get the basics rights – wear comfy clothes, have food and drink to hand (if it's safe to do so), keep warm, find the right work surface and chair, get decent lighting and proper ventilation.

WHEN DISASTER STRIKES
We've all been there. When inspiration fails to come or your work goes horribly, terribly wrong. As children we are often taught to fear getting things wrong but our mistakes teach us much more valuable lessons than our successes. The sooner you get comfortable with making and accepting mistakes, the faster your art or craft will improve.

OPEN TO THE ELEMENTS Potter Emma Lacey works mainly from her studio in North London. Rather than sketch out her designs with pen and paper, she describes her studio as her 'sketchbook', the place where ideas are often formed, practised and perfected in three dimensions.

GET OUT THERE

There's a stereotype that artists prefer to live and work in a reclusive way. Most creatives find the opposite is true. One of the most life-affirming parts about this kind of work is meeting like-minded people, whether it's fellow artists, makers, writers, teachers, gallery owners, patrons and so on. Creative endeavours have the power to inspire other people and uplift them. Get your art or craft out there – it's meant to be seen and enjoyed by others.

WORKTOPS

From chunky workbenches to crafters' tables, wood worktops are eco-friendly, warm to the touch and good looking. Wood's also easy to cut, relatively light and, if sealed properly, water resistant. There was a time when reclaimed timber was a budget option – it's rocketed in price recently, but it's still hard to beat salvaged wood for character and quality. School laboratory worktops, church panelling, mill beams, wide floorboards and railway timber are just a few of the sources of solid and attractive options to explore.

Stainless-steel worktops are great if you're looking for a surface that's waterproof, heatproof and acid resistant – hence its ubiquity in catering. It does scratch easily, but many crafters like the effect this creates over time. It's also often a choice for mechanical repair workbenches as any oil and grease spills won't soak in, so are easily wiped away.

If budgets are tight, a quick and easy workbench can be created from two trestles and laminate fibreboard top. Laminate is easy to wipe clean and high-gloss, so perfect for any projects involving fabric or paper which need to slide around a work surface without catching. If you buy adjustable trestle legs, you also have the option of raising and lowering the worktop height, or tilting it.

You may find that one type of worktop can't satisfy all the different requirements you have – one minute you need a padded surface for pressing fabric, the next a hard surface for craft knife work. Look out for paper-cutting mats, padded fabric covers, wooden chopping boards, stone trivets, carpet underlay and clear acrylic sheets – there are lots of supplementary surfaces you can bring to the table.

WORKADAY SOLUTIONS Not only will it save you money but there's also a creative freedom that comes from using make-shift worktops. Whether it's junkyard doors, old school desks, or trestle legs and an old kitchen worktop, using low-cost materials allows you to get on with being creative without worrying about the scratches and paint splatters.

DESKS

Most creative people don't choose a desk for its ergonomics – we tend to fall in love with the aesthetics first and worry about the bad back later. Everyday office furniture can be soul-sapping in its dullness and low-quality construction, but it is possible to balance style and practicality if you source your desk with a few key points in mind. The first is surface material. Wood, metal, glass, even laminate can look great if you get the colour and finish right – just bear in mind how durable the surface has to be and how likely you are to mark it in everyday practice.

Size is everything. It's frustrating to work at a desk that's too shallow but you can equally go too deep – if you're working on a computer or laptop, for example, the ideal distance between your eyes and the screen is only an arm's length. You don't want to have to overstretch to reach things at the back of your desk. Height-wise, when your hands are resting on the desk your arms should be bent at 90°.

Style-wise, it's up to you. Bureaus are compact, closable and have lots of handy cubbyholes for pens and notebooks – great for writing and small-scale crafts. Corner desks are handy if space is tight but you need a generous work area – you just have to make sure your walls are interesting to look at. Larger, L- and U-shaped desks can accommodate different zones – perfect if you need to separate work activities – but they do eat up floor space, so often a good-sized straight desk with underneath storage is the best overall compromise.

CREATE A VIEWPOINT Whether your desk sits in the middle of your studio or runs along the wall, you'll inevitably have moments when you'll need to sit back and think. A wall full of your favourite images – on a pinboard or framed above your desk – can provide the perfect visual 'horizon' and spur on the creative process.

YI WOTI MA

PARLIAMENT CUT

SEATING

Most artists and crafters tend to move around their studios and sit in different places, or at different heights, so this flexibility can work in your favour when it comes to choosing a chair. Start with a realistic analysis of how you'll be using the space and how long you'll be sitting in one particular place – at an easel, for example, or web surfing. When you really start to unpick your working patterns, you may find that you stand up for a large proportion of the day, or work on the floor. The amount of time you plan on sitting in one place will determine how ergonomic your seating will need to be. If it's less than a few hours a day, the pressure is off to choose something office-based – a barstool, kitchen chair or favourite armchair will be fine for most people. If it's between two and four hours a day, you need to start thinking about chairs that have some level of support, ones designed for occasional home office use. More than four hours sitting in one position and you're into the realm of needing a chair with lumbar support, adjustable seats and armrests and seat padding. Try to vary the different kinds of seating in your studio – a sofa for relaxing, for example, an office chair for desk work and perhaps a saddle stool for painting at an easel (these backless stools are shaped like a horse's saddle, opening up your hip joints and forcing your back into a healthy curve). And remember, we're not really designed to sit still for long periods of time – part of your studio practice should incorporate short, frequent breaks where you stand, walk around and do gentle stretching.

A THOUSAND CHAIRS Whatever your aesthetic, there's a chair to fit. From reclaimed wooden benches to old school seats, architects' chairs to make-shift logs, it's ultimately a balance between comfort and cost. If you can, mix it up – moving from one different seating position to another, and spending periods kneeling or standing, is best for your body. A space to relax is also a must; both Sarah Campbell and Nathalie Lété found spaces in their studios to incorporate sofas and armchairs (overleaf).

LIGHTING

It's not an overstatement to say that lighting can make or break a studio but there's a foolproof combination of lights that will work in practically any studio scenario. If you follow the mantra 'a light to help you walk, a light to help you work and a light just for the hell of it', you can't go far wrong. 'A light to help you walk' – this is the overhead, general light that allows you to wander around your space without crashing into things. It can be an overhead pendant, a set of wall lights, ceiling spotlights or similar but its general aim is to light the room, not you. 'A light to help you work' – this is your task lighting, and whether it's an Anglepoise, a table lamp or a whole series of clip-on spotlights, its one purpose in life is to light you, your hands and your work. You know you've got your task lighting right when you can switch off your overhead light and still work at your desk/workbench effectively. And last, 'a light just for the hell of it' – not compulsory but a great addition to any studio is a light that exists just to make you smile. It doesn't even have to have a particular function, apart from improving your mood, whether it's a string of fairy lights, an illuminated letter, paper lanterns, a neon sign, an extravagant chandelier or a trayful of tealights.

THE HOLY TRINITY OF LIGHTS
The only three light sources you need to worry about in your studio – ambient, task and decorative: ambient lights (such as pendants) illuminate the overall space; task lights (like desk lamps) illuminate your work surface; and decorative lights (such as neon signs or fairy lights) illuminate your mood.

NATURAL
LIGHT

LIGHTEN UP Artificial light can alter how you see colours, so if you need to be accurate there's no substitute for natural light. The top light cast from a skylight (above) provides a generous, diffuse light to work under, even on an overcast day, while industrial windows (opposite), which were originally designed to illuminate a manufacturing space, provide plentiful daylight and wide, uninterrupted views.

No studio is ever perfect. And one of the elements you often have least control over is the amount of natural light. Few of us can afford to create a studio from scratch, with the right amount of windows facing in the right direction, so what can you reasonably do to increase the amount of daylight streaming in?

There are all the obvious things – painting all the walls light colours, hanging up plenty of mirrors, keeping your windows free from heavy curtains and so on – but you also need to think about the contents of your studio. Anything that creates a visual barrier – a screen, partition or internal door – can be glazed or constructed so as to create minimal impact. Clutter can sap the light from a space, so getting your storage and systems right will make a huge difference. And think about floor coverings – gloss-painted floorboards, bright lino and light-coloured concrete will all bounce daylight back whilst still being practical for everyday studio use. You can also make changes to the exterior – glazing the outside door to your studio effectively adds an extra window. Light tubes are a low cost way of popping in roof lights, and skylights provide levels of illumination unmatched by normal windows.

It's also worth adding that simply painting everything brilliant white may not be the best answer. There's an interplay between the colour of your studio and natural light that you want to enhance and maximize. If you face north, for example, instead of brilliant whites introduce off-whites with a hint of warmth to prevent the space feeling too chilly, while south-facing studios can take cooler whites and light off-greys.

STORAGE

OUT IN THE OPEN There's definitely a tendency for artists and craftspeople to create storage that's also display. Part of the pleasure comes from being inspired by the materials of your trade, which are often highly coloured or patterned, and another part comes in being able to easily access the things you need. Open storage also allows you to mix in favourite objects from home or found items that fit your decor.

While some artists, writers and craftspeople thrive in an anarchic workspace – Francis Bacon's studio space was always fantastically cluttered – most creative people need at least some semblance of order to work effectively. Being organized doesn't have to be sterile, and in many ways it frees up your time to concentrate on the thing that really matters i.e. being creative. Any work you produce in your studio – whether it's a kitchen table or a dedicated space – will ultimately be a reflection of your environment. If you want frenzied or unruly work, a disordered studio will do the trick. If you want something more focused, you'll need to organize the tools of your trade.

With a studio, however, storage is also part of the aesthetic. The boxes and baskets you choose, the shelves you build, the things you stack in neat piles, all come together to create a look that will hopefully inspire your work. Keeping things hidden away might work for some items, but others will need to be visually available at all times; like a chef choosing ingredients in a fruit market, the creative process often involves visually picking through and pondering the materials at your disposal.

It's interesting that so many studio spaces have open or see-through storage. There's a good reason for this. Not only does it keep all your materials neat and tidy, but it also allows your imagination to be fired up by their colours, forms and textures. And, as with any other element in a studio, your storage choices should fit your aesthetic. From the industrial chic of galvanized metal boxes to the sweet-shop cheeriness of glass jars, the options can be both useful and decorative. Necessity is the mother of invention and creative people often don't have the budgets to splash out on expensive storage. The result, happily, is that artists and

craftspeople have come up with some ingenious ways to repurpose kitchen and bedroom storage to suit the studio environment. From plastic shoe caddies to vegetable racks, kitchen-roll holders to spice racks, lots of work-a-day options translate into practical studio storage.

When you're planning your studio you need to ask yourself some basic practical questions: how often do I need to access or use this particular item? Do I want to be able to see it or read its label at a glance? How important is it that my materials are categorized? Take a sewing studio, for example; so many small and fiddly raw materials to contend with means that small, labelled, compartmentalized storage often works better than large, open boxes.

SORTED STORAGE Let your materials dictate your choice of storage; micro components need small jars and miniature drawers while bulkier craft supplies often suit large shelved cupboards and stacked boxes.

STUDIO STORAGE RULES

- **More is good.** Better the storage, better the workspace.

- **Think floor to ceiling.** Keep heavy materials and tools low down.

- **Create clear categories.** Sort into groups. Divide, sub-divide.

- **Label everything.** Use stickers, polaroids, marker pens, laundry labels, luggage tags.

- **Keep often-used things close by.** Store things where you'll utilize them.

- **Make it pretty.** Use storage that not only works, but looks good.

- **Kid proof.** Paints, solvents, glues, varnishes – lock away toxics.

SHELVES

You almost can't have too many shelves in a studio. They're a brilliantly flexible form of organization – part storage, part showing off – and they'll fit into all but the most awkward spaces. Before you start drilling holes in every vertical surface, however, just bear in mind a few practical issues. One is load – how much weight are you going to expect your shelf to bear? We're all guilty of asking a little too much of our humble shelves, so over-engineer any solutions you come up with. Deeper wall fixings, extra brackets, X-braces, thicker shelves, safety straps for free-standing shelves – all sensible options if they're going to carry significant loads. Vary their depth and height for flexibility and choice and, if it's practical, incorporate adjustable brackets. When it comes to materials, you need to think about its propensity to flex under weight. Comparing materials of the same thickness, particleboard and MDF will sag more easily than solid wood or thick ply. And plan the depth of your shelves depending on what you'll store on them. Fabric samples, small baskets, box files, letter trays, laptops and many other mid-sized studio basics will fit neatly onto a 40-cm (15½-inch) deep shelf.

For all the appeal of digital information, nothing quite beats books and magazines for firing your imagination. Alongside the convenience of having these physical resources to hand, there's also an undeniable pleasure to be had from having a personal library shelves to look at and peruse at your own pace. From art books to consumer magazines, artists and craftspeople regularly use reference material to inspire their work and it can be an important element in a studio. Books are often beautiful things in their own right – a shelf full of colourful spines is a delight – so open shelving is always a great way to introduce order and visual appeal. Anything valuable or vulnerable needs to be kept in a glazed cupboard, and unruly stacks of magazines might be better corralled into box files or crates on castors if they're threatening to spill over onto work areas. Built-in bookcases are great space in-fillers, often where other pieces of furniture can't be accommodated, or double up and use your bookcases as room dividers or 'legs' for a worktop. Face out book storage (where you see the covers) can create an arresting display, but it does eat up space, so is best kept for favourite volumes.

MAKE IT HAPPEN If you can't find a shelf that fits your requirements, make one. Sometimes the best solutions are the bespoke ones; artist illustrator Olaf Hajek, who describes himself as a 'book addict', designed his own bookshelves to accommodate all his paints and reference materials (opposite), while designer Nathalie Lété uses detachable cubes that can be stacked and restacked at will (above).

WALL TREATMENTS

WHAT'S GOING ON INSIDE

The walls of a studio are often the outward expression of what's going on inside a creative brain. Some are chaotic: walls plastered with images and inspirational quotes; tools and artwork hung in a haphazard way; layers upon layers of ideas and work in progress. Other studio walls are neatly ordered, gallery-like, or even totally bare and free from distraction – some people find they need visual 'peace' to work effectively.

On a practical level, there are some common factors to consider when you're planning your studio walls. These are colour, texture and material. There's been reams written about colour and its effect on mood and creativity; the reality is that colour is experienced on so many different levels – physiologically, culturally and psychologically – that it's over-simplistic to say, for example, that painting your studio walls red will energize you while black walls will sap your spirits. If you need plenty of natural light for your work, it makes sense to opt for whites and pales, but on a creative level only you can choose the colour that will help you think and work. As with all creative ventures, you'll only discover the truth by experimenting. Visit places with wall colours that switch you on; hang fabric on the wall to test a shade you like; paint one wall and experience it at different times of the day. There'll also be a functional element to your colour choice – does the wall need to be a clean white back-drop for your work, for example, or double-up as a chalkboard?

Texture also comes into play. If your craft is a messy one, smooth surfaces are obviously easier to wipe down than rough, but beyond that different wall textures create markedly different effects. Rough-hewn timber lends an instantly warm, rustic feel to a space, for example, while aluminium sheets are perfect for a more industrial look. Artists often like a variety of textures, enjoying the interplay between different surfaces – bare brick on one wall, for example, and smooth painted board on another. Acoustically, different textures create different effects. Fabric or timber-lined walls tend to absorb sound, for instance, while hard shiny surfaces such as metal or bare concrete bounce noise around.

PEGBOARDS
AND
PINBOARDS

IN PLAIN SIGHT Pinboards, pegboards and other kinds of inspiration boards are the beating heart of a studio. Not only do they provide a useful surface for storing tools and materials, but they're also microcosms of creativity. Quotes, images, sketches, colour swatches, works in progress – these create a mini collage of your thoughts and work practice. Judit Just's board (above) is a kaleidoscope of yarn, weaving samples and images; Lisa Congdon's pegboard (opposite) keeps her tools safely stowed.

When you are working on a creative project, the thinking and looking stage is an important part of your practice. You need time to reflect on what you're doing and get ideas from the things that surround you. Inspiration boards are critical to this process in so many ways – they create a two-way dialogue – you feed your inspiration board with newly discovered clippings, images and quotes and, in return, your inspiration board feeds you back. It gives you insight and motivation when the going gets tough, it cheers you up when you're having a low moment, and it reflects and bolsters your creative talent – it reminds you what you are doing and why. How you organize your inspiration board is up to you – some people love the patchwork collage effect, multiple images plastered over each other. Others like a more considered, pared-down approach, choosing a few select images and giving each one plenty of visual space.

Pegboards are essentially for hanging things from but they can also double as a pinning area – use bulldog clips, large paperclips, strings between two pegs or washi tape to attach images rather than drawing pins. This has the added benefit of creating an inspiration wall that can not only accommodate images but also physical things such as little mementos, swatches, ribbons, tapes, small tools, clipboards and other things hung from its surface.

Pinboards are also a studio favourite. Cork is traditionally the base material, but cellulose fibreboard will also do the trick and has enough 'give' to make it suitable for tacks – you can always cover your board with a favourite fabric or thick wallpaper if you want to add colour and pattern. Drawing pins (or push pins) come in all shapes and sizes – from tiny paper planes to cress seeds, ladybirds to lollipops. For the unstoppable crafter, there's even the option of pimping your own pins – a glue gun, some flat-headed drawing pins, and the sky's the limit. From googly eyes to spotty buttons, toy soldiers to Barbie shoes, it seems there are few things that can't be fixed to the end of a pin.

Padded boards can be a bit restrictive for studios as the only way to attach images is to tuck them under the crisscross strings – fine for organizing the occasional correspondence but not massively useful for lots of cuttings and scraps. Metallic noticeboards, however, are a great option if you don't like fiddly pins and prefer holding things with magnets. You don't even have to buy a board – a tin of magnetic paint allows you to paint your own magnetic surface on any flat area. It can also be used as an undercoat, so you can add a topcoat in your favourite shade and still keep the magnetic properties.

MOOD WALL Paula Mills' everchanging inspiration board allows her to be surrounded by the things she loves, be it a specific colour combination or a piece of hand lettering.

SCREENS AND DIVIDERS

When it comes to using a studio, many people find they like to compartmentalize their space. This can be practical – one area for messy activities, for example, and another for clean work. But as often as not, the reason is more instinctive – it can help your practice if you feel that different work areas are separated off, either from living spaces or from each other. Artists' studios, for instance, often have areas for hanging work and other areas for making it. If you work from home, a screen can help you cut off from the domestic arena. Or, if you have an openplan space and it doesn't feel right, creating smaller, more intimate working spaces is often the solution.

You can achieve this in so many ways: a simple stud wall, hospital screens on castors, a vast bookcase or open storage unit, a curtain or paper screen. Think about how permanent you want the division to be – it's harder to change the position of a stud wall or curtain track than to push around a folding screen on wheels. If light is an issue, consider constructing a half-wall or 'pony wall', which divides the space but only up to waist height. Translucent screens, sheer curtains and glass partitions will also section off spaces without stealing any light. Large plants in tubs – such as long-leaved figs or house palms – can act as a screen and also add a whole host of other benefits, visual and health-wise.

PERFECT PARTITION Screens can reveal as much as they hide. Here, Claire Basler's folding partition not only divides a large studio into distinct sections, but it's also a beautiful work of art in itself, reflecting the light and giving a tantalizing glimpse of the studio space beyond.

DRYING
SPACES

Lots of creative pursuits need drying spaces. Whether it's an oil canvas or a hand-thrown pot, the drying stage is often critical and needs somewhere clean, dust-free and, if possible, out of the way. Simple arrangements, such as washing lines with pegs or string and bulldog clips, are ideal for small sketches or paintings, and can easily be strung between two high points. Laundry racks and maids' dollies are also good options if space is tight as you can mount them at ceiling height. Circular peg racks are particularly handy for multiple, small projects, such as lino cuts, rubber stamps or woodblock prints. Larger, wet canvases can be dried in specially designed slotted boxes (wet painting carriers), racks, pull-out drawers, on the wall, open shelving or easels, depending on practicalities.

Drying clay is a critical step before firing and you need lots of open shelves so air can circulate freely around each pot. Slow, even drying is best, so avoid humidity, big temperature fluctuations and sources of heat. Flat clay objects (such as tiles) are best laid on racks, so both top and bottom surfaces have a chance to dry out. For other crafts, if you're doing anything that involves paints or glues that need to dry out, check whether you need special ventilation; most craft glues are PVA based and non-toxic but certain adhesives such as spray glues, superglues and epoxy resin all give off harmful fumes, so they'll need to be away from your working space while they are curing.

DIRECTORY

STYLE GUIDES

Pages 34–35: *amara.com; dotcomgiftshop.com; fermliving. com; hay.dk; howkapow.com; made. com; my-furniture.com; habitat.co.uk; talkingtables.co.uk; oliverbonas.com; dan300.com.au; blockdesign.co.uk*
Page 46–47: *amara.com; einrichten-design.de; fermliving. com; florafurniture.co.uk; made. com; theoldcinema.co.uk; loaf.com; www.harleyandlola.co.uk*
Pages 60–61: *rossandbrownhome. co.uk; amara.com; anthropologie. eu; atkinandthyme.co.uk; homesense. com; looptheloop.co.uk; miafleur.com; outthereinteriors.com; sainsburys.co.uk; wildandwolf.com*
Pages 78–79: *alexanderandpearl.co.uk; furnish.co.uk; red5.co.uk; theoldcinema.co.uk; cribdeluxe.co.uk*
Pages 98–99: *alexanderandpearl.co.uk; caravanstyle.com; deborahbowness.com; heals.co.uk; homebarnshop.co.uk; one.world; vintagematters.co.uk; deepuddy.co.uk*

UK

ANTHROPOLOGIE
Joyously bohemian stationery and home decor
anthropologie.com

HABITAT
Reliably chic storage, desks, seating and shelves
habitat.co.uk

HUS & HEM
A smorgasbord of Scandi studio furniture and accessories
husandhem.co.uk

ROOM DIVIDERS
Every imaginable type of folding screens and partitions for studios
roomdividersuk.co.uk

SCREWFIX
DIY destination for tool storage, metal racks and shelves, lockers and cabinets
screwfix.com

GREAT ART
Phenomenally comprehensive range of art and craft materials
greatart.co.uk

ROCKETT ST GEORGE
Quirky, eclectic interiors emporium – rugs, lighting and furniture
rockettstgeorge.co.uk

TINSMITHS
Craft-led online shop selling fabrics, artists' prints and furniture
tinsmiths.co.uk

DECORATOR'S NOTEBOOK
Home and office wares with an ethical, global ethos
decoratorsnotebook.co.uk

THE MINT LIST
Vintage storage, retro workdesks, upcycled pieces
themintlist.com

MADE
Original, design-led furniture and lighting straight from the manufacturer
made.com

LAMP AND LIGHT
Lights and lamps for virtually every corner of your studio
lampandlight.co.uk

GRACE & GLORY
Cool, edited selection of pegboards, wirework shelves and lighting
graceandgloryhome.co.uk

SALVO
Reclamation nirvana – includes 'For Sale' and 'Wanted' sections and directory of yards
salvo.co.uk

FOX & STAR
Unique stationery, planners and endless rolls of washi tape
thefoxandstar.co.uk

PAPERCHASE
Bright, cheery stationery, craft supplies and storage
paperchase.co.uk

LAWRENCE
Drying racks, easels, plan chests, craft tables for the serious artist
lawrence.co.uk

IKEA
The mothership for modular storage, trestles and cheap storage
ikea.com

AUSTRALIA

KITSCH PLEASE
Online marketplace for high quality vintage homewares and furniture
kitschplease.com.au

STONE PONY
Industrial-inspired furniture and accents
stonepony.com.au

DIRECT OFFICE FURNITURE
No-frills filing cabinets, chairs, desks and a useful second-hand office furniture section
directoffice.com.au

SAFARI LIVING
Global selection of textiles and furnishings from new designers and established brands
safariliving.com

BUNNINGS
No-nonsense pegboards, pinboards and chalkboards
bunnings.com.au

FENTON & FENTON
Vintage furniture, vivid textiles and one-off curios from around the globe
fentonandfenton.com.au

WEST ELM
'Mid-century modern' home office furniture and decor
westelm.com.au

CULT DESIGN
Ice cool selection of modern and Danish office furniture
cultdesign.com.au

VAMPT VINTAGE DESIGN
Carefully curated vintage desks, lighting and storage
vamptvintagedesign.com

THE ART SHOP
Easels, art materials, brushes and canvases by the bucketful
theartshop.com.au

CRAFT ONLINE
All thing crafty, tools and paper
craftonline.com.au

US

ALL MODERN
Modern great-looking studio essentials including lamps, rugs and storage
allmodern.com

BLU DOT
Chic, clean-lined home office furniture including task chairs and lighting
bludot.com

CRATE & BARREL
Simple, well-designed pieces including home office furniture and storage
crateandbarrel.com

KNOLL
Smart, ergonomic home studio solutions including chairs and worktables
knoll.com

LULU & GEORGIA
Glamorous, stylish, colourful home decor with a vintage edge
luluandgeorgia.com

POTTERY BARN
Reliably chic and affordable homewares and ways to get organized
potterybarn.com

REJUVENATION
Vintage and antique-inspired goodies including industrial lighting and storage
rejuvenation.com

SCHOOLHOUSE ELECTRIC & SUPPLY CO.
Vintage-led, stylish furniture, office supplies and lighting
schoolhouseelectric.com

SERENA & LILY
Elegant, relaxed furniture including desks, shelves, lighting and accessories
serenaandlily.com

USM
Ultra cool modular furniture including desks, credenzas, sideboards and storage
usm.com

CREATIVE PEOPLE IN THIS BOOK

ARIELE ALASKO
arielealasko.com

MARI ANDREWS
mariandrews.com

KATRIN BÅÅTH
katrinb.se

CLAIRE BASLER
clairebasler.com

HOLLY BECKER
decor8blog.com

ILARIA CHIARATTI BONOMI
idainteriorlifestyle.com

JULIA BOSTOCK
juliabostock.com

SARAH CAMPBELL
sarahcampbelldesigns.com

LISA CONGDON
lisacongdon.com

CATHERINE DERKSEMA
printscharming.com.au

AGATA DIMMICH
passionshake.com

BENJAMIN EDMONDS
blok-knives.co.uk

LINDA FELCEY
lindafelcey.com

NICOLAS FLACHOT
kidimo.com

NICK FOUQUET
nickfouquet.com

TENKA GAMMELGAARD
tenka.dk

HELENA GAVSHON
helenagavshon.com

SYLWIA GERVAIS
syllovesshabby.blogspot.com

OLAF HAJEK
olafhajek.de

CADENCE HAYS
instagram.com/thewhiitehouse

MARK HEARLD
stjudesgallery.co.uk

KIEL JAMES PATRICK &
SARAH VICKERS
kjp.com

INGRID JANSEN
woodwoolstool.com

JUDIT JUST
etsy.com/uk/people/jujujust

EMMA LACEY
emmalacey.com

PENNY LEAVER GREEN
pennyleavergreen.co.uk

NATHALIE LÉTÉ
nathalie-lete.com

AMY LORD & REBEKAH WHITNEY
lordwhitney.co.uk

LISE MEUNIER
lise-meunier.blogspot.com

MAX McMURDO
maxmcmurdo.co.uk

PAULA MILLS
paulamillsillustration.com

MARTIN O'NEILL
cutitout.co.uk

SHAUNA RICHARDSON
shaunarichardson.com

GAVIN ROOKLEDGE
rooksbooks.com

HEATHER ROSS
heatherross.ca

AARON RUFF
digbyandiona.com

EMILY SUTTON
emillustrates.com

SALLY TAYLOR
sallytaylor.net

CHARIS WILLIAMS
chariswilliams.co.uk

PICTURE CREDITS

Page; 1: Sandra Juto (copyright © Jacqui Small LLP)

Page 2: Alun Callender (copyright © Jacqui Small LLP)

Pages 4–5: Holly Becker decor8blog.com

Page 6: Narratives, Alun Callender

Pages 8–9: Sara Landstedt

Page 10: Yossy Arefi

Pages 12–13: Lord Whitney

Page 15: Janis Nicolay (copyright © Jacqui Small LLP)

Pages 16–17: Claire Basler

Pages 18–19: Sara Landstedt (studio of Katrin Bååth)

Page 20 left: living4media, Andrew Boyd

Pages 20–21 centre: Alun Callender (copyright © Jacqui Small LLP) (studio of Sarah Campbell)

Page 21 right: Rachel Smith

Page 22: Sylwia Gervais

Page 23: Judit Just

Pages 24–29: Alun Callender (copyright © Jacqui Small LLP)

Pages 30–31: Tigs Maeallan

Pages 32–33: Judit Just

Pages 34–35: amara.com; dotcomgiftshop.com; fermliving.com; hay.dk; howkapow.com; made.com; my-furniture.com; habitat.co.uk; talkingtables.co.uk; oliverbonas.com; dan300.com.au; blockdesign.co.uk

Page 36 left: Pia Jane Bijkerk, living4media

Pages 36–37 centre: Taverne

Page 37 right: Taverne

Pages 38–39: Sara Landstedt

Page 40: Idha Lindhag

Page 41: House of Pictures

Pages 42–45: Sara Landstedt

Pages 46–47: amara.com; einrichten-design. de; fermliving.com; florafurniture.co.uk; made.com; theoldcinema.co.uk; loaf.com; harleyandlola.co.uk

Page 48 left: Alun Callender

Pages 48–49 centre: Claire Basler

Page 49 right: Cadence Hays

Page 50 left: Claire Basler

Page 50 top right: Heather Ross

Pages 51–55: Claire Basler

Pages 56– 59: Alun Callender

Pages 60–61: rossandbrownhome.co.uk;

amara.com; anthropologie.eu; atkinandthyme.co.uk; homesense. com; looptheloop.co.uk; miafleur.com; outthereinteriors.com; sainsburys.co.uk; wildandwolf.com

Page 62 left: Rachel Kara (copyright © Jacqui Small LLP) (studio of Catherine Derksema)

Pages 62–63 centre: Catherine Gratwicke, living4media

Page 63 right: Victoria Harley (copyright © Jacqui Small LLP) (studio of Benjamin Edmonds/Blok Knives)

Page 64: Victoria Harley (copyright © Jacqui Small LLP) (studio of Benjamin Edmonds/Blok Knives)

Page 65: Joanna Maclennan (copyright © Jacqui Small LLP) (studio of Nathalie Lété),

Pages 66–69: Brian Ferry

Pages 70–73: Rachel Kara (copyright © Jacqui Small LLP)

Pages 74–77: Victoria Harley (copyright © Jacqui Small LLP) (studio of Benjamin Edmonds/Blok Knives)

Pages 78–79: alexanderandpearl.co.uk; furnish.co.uk; red5.co.uk; theoldcinema. co.uk; cribdeluxe.co.uk

Page 80 left: Joanna Maclennan (copyright © Jacqui Small LLP) (studio of Nathalie Lété),

Pages 80–81 centre: Alun Callender (copyright © Jacqui Small LLP)

Page 81 right: Alun Callender (copyright © Jacqui Small LLP)

Page 82 left & right: Alun Callender (copyright © Jacqui Small LLP)

Pages 83–87: Joanna Maclennan (copyright © Jacqui Small LLP)

Pages 88–97: Alun Callender (copyright © Jacqui Small LLP)

Pages 98–99: alexanderandpearl.co.uk; caravanstyle.com; deborahbowness.com; heals.co.uk; homebarnshop.co.uk; one. world; vintagematters.co.uk; deepuddy.co.uk

Pages 100–101: Yossy Arefi (studio of Ariele Alasko)

Page 102: Cadence Hays

Pages 102–103 centre: James Balston

Page 103 right: Joanna Maclennan (copyright © Jacqui Small LLP)

Page 104: Cadence Hays

Page 105: Yossy Arefi (studio of Ariele Alasko)

Pages 106–109: Joanna Maclennan (copyright © Jacqui Small LLP)

Pages 110–113: Yossy Arefi

Page 114 left: Ingrid Jansen

Pages 114–115 centre: Galen Oakes

Page 115 right: Polly Eltes

Page 116: Rachel Kara (copyright © Jacqui Small LLP) (studio of Catherine Derksema)

Page 117 top: Polly Eltes (studio of Helena Gavshon)

Page 117 bottom: James Balston

Pages 118–21: Galen Oakes

Pages 122–25: James Balston

Pages 126–29: Polly Eltes

Page 130 left: Emilio R. Ferrer, living4media

Pages 130–31centre: Victoria Harley (copyright © Jacqui Small LLP)

Page 131: Sandra Juto (copyright © Jacqui Small LLP)

Page 132 top: Sandra Juto (copyright © Jacqui Small LLP) (studio of Olaf Hajek)

Page 132 bottom: Sally Anne Hartwell (studio of Paula Mills)

Page 133: living4media, Cecilia Möller

Page 134: Janis Nicolay (copyright © Jacqui Small LLP) (studio of Lisa Congdon)

Page 135: living4media, Jalag, Olaf Szczepaniak

Pages 136–37: Victoria Harley (copyright © Jacqui Small LLP)

Pages 138–43: Janis Nicolay (copyright © Jacqui Small LLP)

Pages 144–47: Sibila Savage

Pages 148–51: Sandra Juto (copyright © Jacqui Small LLP)

Page 152 left: Agata Dimmich

Pages 152–53 centre: Lord Whitney

Page 153 right: Janis Nicolay (copyright © Jacqui Small LLP)

Page 154: Sara Landstedt

Page 155: Ilaria Chiaratti Bonomi

Page 156: Julia Bostock

Page 157: Holly Becker decor8blog.com

Pages 158–61:Janis Nicolay (copyright © Jacqui Small LLP)

Pages 162–65: Holly Becker decor8blog. com (portrait of Holly Becker page 165 Anouschka Rokebrand)

Pages 166–69: Julia Bostock

Page 170 left: Charis Williams

Pages 170–71 centre: Frederic Lucano

Page 171 right: Simon Brown (copyright © Jacqui Small LLP)

Page 172: James Balston

Page 173: Victoria Harley (copyright © Jacqui Small LLP)

Page 174: Simon Brown (copyright © Jacqui Small LLP)

Page 175: Heather Ross

Pages 176–79: Frederic Lucano

Pages 180–81: Charis Williams

Pages 182–83: Lord Whitney

Page 185: Lord Whitney

Pages 186–87: James Balston

Pages 188–89: Heather Ross

Page 191: Yeshen Venema

Page 192: Tigs Maeallan (studio of Paula Mills)

Page 193: Rachel Kara (copyright © Jacqui Small LLP) (studio of Catherine Derksema)

Page 194: living4media, Jansje Klazinga

Page 195: Paula Mills

Page 196 left: Rachel Kara (copyright © Jacqui Small LLP) (studio of Catherine Derksema)

Page 196 right: Victoria Harley (copyright © Jacqui Small LLP) (studio of Sally Taylor)

Page 197 left: James Balston

Page 197 right: Victoria Harley (copyright © Jacqui Small LLP) (studio of Ben Edmonds/ Blok Knives)

Page 198: Alun Callender (copyright © Jacqui Small LLP)

Page 199: Joanna Maclennan (copyright © Jacqui Small LLP)

Page 200 top: James Balston

Page 200 bottom: Victoria Harley (copyright © Jacqui Small LLP) (studio of Ben Edmonds/ Blok Knives)

Page 201: Frederic Lucano

Page 202: Alun Callender (copyright © Jacqui Small LLP) (studio of Mark Hearld)

Page 203: Sara Landstedt

Page 204 left: Narratives, Brent Darby

Page 204 right: Taverne

Page 205: Taverne

Page 206: Ingrid Jansen

Page 207: GAP Interiors, Amanda Turner

Page 208: Sandra Juto (copyright © Jacqui Small LLP)

Page 209: Joanna Maclennan (copyright © Jacqui Small LLP)

Page 210: Taverne

Page 211: Narratives, Brent Darby

Page 212: Judit Just

Page 213: Janis Nicolay (copyright © Jacqui Small LLP)

Pages 214–15: Sally Anne Hartwell

Pages 216–17: Claire Basler

Page 218: Yeshen Venema

Page 219: Victoria Harley (copyright © Jacqui Small LLP)

Front endpapers: Frederic Lucano (studio of Nicolas Flachot)

Back endpapers: Alun Callender (copyright © Jacqui Small LLP) (studio of Martin O'Neill)

Front cover: Pia Jane Bijkerk, living4media

Back cover: Yossy Arefi

ACKNOWLEDGEMENTS

As always, huge thanks to the amazing team of in-house staff and freelancers involved in making this book come to life, including Jacqui, Jo, Eszter, Sian, Rachel, Caroline, Helen, Joe and Marta.

Special thanks goes to D for his *très bon* translating.